Case Studies of
Minority Student Placement
in Special Education

Case Studies of Minority Student Placement in Special Education

BETH HARRY
JANETTE KLINGNER
ELIZABETH CRAMER

with

KEITH M. STURGES AND ROBERT F. MOORE

TEACHERS COLLEGE PRESS

TEACHERS COLLEGE | COLUMBIA UNIVERSITY

NEW YORK AND LONDON

Published by Teachers College Press, 1234 Amsterdam Avenue, New York, NY 10027

Library of Congress Cataloging-in-Publication Data

Harry, Beth.
  Case studies of minority student placement in special education / Beth Harry, Janette Klingner, Elizabeth Cramer ; with Keith M. Sturges and Robert F. Moore.
    p. cm.
  Includes bibliographical references and index.
  ISBN 978-0-8077-4761-2 (pbk. : alk. paper)
  1. Special education—United States—Case studies. 2. Children with disabilities—Education—United States—Case studies. 3. Discrimination in education—United States—Case studies. 4. Minorities—Education—United States—Case studies. 5. Educational equalization—United States. I. Klingner, Janette K. II. Cramer, Elizabeth P. III. Sturges, Keith M. IV. Title.
  LC3981.H355 2006
  371.9089—dc22

                                                                          2006103290

ISBN 978-0-8077-4761-2 (paper)

Printed on acid-free paper

Manufactured in the United States of America

Contents

Preface: The Issue, the Research, and the Setting   **vii**

Acknowledgments   **xi**

PART I: THE DISPROPORTIONATE PLACEMENT OF MINORITY STUDENTS IN SPECIAL EDUCATION

1. **The Social Construction of High-Incidence Disabilities**   **3**

2. **The "Judgment" Categories: Dilemmas of Definition, Assessment, and Placement**   **8**

PART II: CASE STUDIES

3. **Emotional/Behavior Disorder or Attention Deficit Hyperactivity Disorder?**   **21**

   Robert: *"I'm a gangsta, tha's why!"*

4. **Emotional/Behavior Disorder or Gifted?**   **29**

   Kanita: *"There's nothing wrong with her, she just wants her momma"*

5. **Emotional/Behavior Disorder, Learning Disability, or Just Sensitive?**   **38**

   Germaine: *"Why you looking at me?"*

6. **Emotional/Behavior Disorder or Learning Disability?**   **46**

   Matthew and Austin: *"I have a dream . . ."*

7. Emotional/Behavior Disorder, Learning Disability, or English-Language Learner? 61

  Edith: *"She's NOT handicap!"*

8. Attention Deficit Hyperactivity Disorder, Emotional/Behavior Disorder, or Learning Disability? 71

  Paul: *"I don't want this case to go EBD."*

9. Educable Mentally Retarded, English-Language Learner, or Ignored? 79

  Clementina: *"I don't want to do no work!"*

10. Educable Mentally Retarded, English-Language Learner, or Ignored? 87

  Bartholomew: *"SO?"*

11. Learning Disabled or Absent? 92

  Miles: *"I can add and subtract just like them."*

12. Learning Disabled or Absent? 99

  Anita: *"I'm tired of this school and all their mistakes!"*

13. Learning Disabled or Low Achiever? 108

  Marc: *"He's a quiet person in class; he's just slow."*

14. Between the Cracks? 113

  Taddeus: *"He can fix anything!"*

Epilogue: The Tyranny of the Norm 117

References 119

Index 121

About the Authors 131

Preface:
The Issue, the Research,
and the Setting

In this book we use ethnographic case studies to address the issue of the disproportionate placement of ethnic minority students in special education programs. As a companion book to *Why Are So Many Minority Students in Special Education?* the case studies provide a personalized and detailed view of the broader and more general report in the first book. Ideally, for graduate students, the two books should be used in tandem to present readers with the richness of the study and the complexity of the issue of disproportionality. However, the case studies could be used on their own, and we envision that this would be very appropriate for undergraduate students in general and special education, and especially for dual-certification programs.

The case studies bring to life the real children, school personnel, and family members whose voices reflect widely varying views and interpretations of the issue of minority placement in high-incidence disability categories. The perspectives of all stakeholders are faithfully represented, showing the tremendous complexity of the issues and the challenges faced by professionals, family members, and children. At the end of each case study, challenging questions and scenarios provide instructors with thoughtful alternatives for follow-up activities and further study.

Part I of this casebook will provide readers with adequate understanding of the definitional, assessment, and placement dilemmas surrounding each disability category and the placement process as a whole. In Part II, the 12 cases are organized to highlight two central issues: the challenge of distinguishing disability from children's opportunity to learn, and the ambiguity surrounding the selection of one specific category to represent a child's "disability." Our overarching concern is, Is the use of these categories valid? Must we require them for the provision of special education services?

DATA SOURCES

These 12 case studies emerged from 4 years of research, whose findings are described in detail in the companion book. Of these 12 students, 11 were "full case study" students, whom we followed for at least 3 years. The other represents a student who did not qualify for special services and on whom we collected considerable data over a period of 1 year. In the first 3 years an ethnographic approach was used. In the 4th year, we collected data only on the academic scores and overall status of the children in their special education placements. In all, we collected the following data:

- 8–12 classroom observations for each child
- observations of assessments and child study team (CST) and placement conferences wherever possible
- at least one interview with a parent/guardian
- records from cumulative files, including psychological evaluation, social history, individualized education program (IEP), current standardized-test scores, report cards, home language survey where appropriate, teacher observation checklist, and referrals for disciplinary action
- work samples
- administration of a school attitude survey and a Woodcock Johnson evaluation to ascertain current reading and math grade equivalents
- interviews with relevant school personnel, including school psychologists, referring teachers, special education teachers, and school counselors

THE SCHOOLS

There were 12 schools involved in the 3 years of research. Upon selecting our case study students, however, we included 9 schools, based on our analysis of which children would provide the best exemplars of the dilemmas of disproportionality. Table 1 provides the basic demographic features of each school. Throughout the text, we will use the more general term *Black* to encompass African, Haitian, and Caribbean Americans unless it is important to distinguish ethnicity. Also, although we acknowledge that Latino is preferred in many locations, for persons from Spanish-speaking territories we will use the term *Hispanic* since it is the commonly used term in the school district where the study was conducted. The nine schools can be described as falling into four demographic clusters:

1. Five inner-city, old neighborhoods, serving primarily African American; Haitian; and to a lesser extent, Hispanic students. Our analysis of the quality of the schools indicated that these all had an imbalance of weak teachers.
2. One school in a low-income suburb that included children of migrant agricultural workers of mostly Mexican origin and African American families of low income. Our analysis of the quality of the schools indicated that this school had an imbalance of weak teachers.
3. Two low- to middle-income neighborhoods, one predominantly Hispanic and one predominantly African American. Our analysis of the quality of these schools indicated that the former school had a majority of strong teachers while the latter had a fairly even spread of weak to strong teachers.
4. One suburban, relatively new school, serving a population of high-income, predominantly Anglo and Hispanic students, with a minority of African American students bused in from a low-income neighborhood, through a desegregation court order. Our analysis of the quality of this school indicated a high majority of strong teachers.

Table I. School Demographics: Ethnicity, Free/Reduced-Price Lunch, and Disability Rates

School	Percentage of Ethnicity of Students *			Free/ Reduced-Price Lunch	Percentage of Educable Mental Retardation	Percentage of Emotional Behavior Disorder	Percentage of Learning Disability
	White	Black	Hispanic				
Bay Vista	8	1	90	68.7			6.6
Sunnybrook	55	17	23	18.5			4.1
Clearwater	3	92	3	70.1	0.2		4.1
Centerville	0	99	1	97.1	7		9.8
Palm Grove	0	89	10	98.9	0.5		6.8
Creekside	0	92	8	97.2	0.1	0.01	3.5
Beecher Stowe	1	69	29	98.4	2.6		4.2
Mabel Oakes	2	56	42	99.0		0.1	4.4
South Park	2	79	19	98.3	0.5	0.3	5.8

* Percentages do not necessarily add up to 100 because in certain instances ethnicities were present that were not specified in the school district figures.

Acknowledgments

The first two authors of this casebook were the coprincipal investigators on the Office of Special Education Programs (OSEP)-funded research grant that formed the basis of this and the companion book, *Why Are So Many Minority Students in Special Education? Understanding Race and Disability in Schools.* The third author of this volume, Elizabeth Cramer, was a graduate assistant on the project and was instrumental in coauthoring these case reports. Keith Sturges was the project coordinator for the research and Robert Moore was the project's in-house consultant.

In addition, the research was supported by a team of data collectors, whose careful field work contributed to the individual cases. In the writing of the cases, we specifically acknowledge the work of Juliet Hart and Cassaundra Wimes. We also give special thanks to the assistants who were engaged in the second part of the study, which focused on intensive collection of data on individual cases: Sherene McKesey, Patricia Stevens, and Sylvia Gutierrez. In addition, we thank Josefa Rascón, Thaissa Champagne, Heather Rutland, Aileen Angulo, Tony Ford, Christina Herrera, Tamara Celestin, and Jennifer Dorce.

PART I

The Disproportionate Placement of Minority Students in Special Education

The Social Construction
of High-Incidence Disabilities

We argue in this casebook that disability is a socially constructed concept. What does the term *social construction* mean? To state that a phenomenon is socially constructed is not to deny its existence. Rather, the term is used to emphasize that society, or groups within a society, agree to attribute certain meanings to the phenomenon. In the case of disabilities, the social construction argument does not deny that a range of abilities exists among children. That range, however, represents a continuum of cognitive and behavioral strengths and limitations that may be the result of several factors, including inherent dispositions, personality, family nurturance, and opportunities to acquire valued school knowledge and behaviors. When we look at a child's learning or behavioral characteristics and interpret them as resulting from a "disability," we are applying a judgment that the point on the continuum at which the individual's achievement falls is sufficiently different from an accepted norm to be considered pathological. It is like an impairment that is part of the individual's personal makeup. This notion of disability or impairment forms the centerpiece of our society's official view of disability under the Individuals with Disabilities Education Improvement Act (IDEA) (PL 108-446, 2004).

Under IDEA, there are three disability categories that are most easily understood as social constructions because they are based on individual judgments about where normalcy ends and disability begins: educable mental retardation (EMR), emotional/behavioral disorder (EBD), and specific learning disability (SLD or LD). Individuals classified in these categories seldom display characteristics that can be verified as pathological through any system of objective analysis. There are seldom any clear biological characteristics that can be specified and measured. Although we view these features as pathological, the interpretation is essentially based on societal norms for development and learning, not on measurable facts. We must note here that the category attention deficit hyperactivity disorder (ADHD), while not recognized by IDEA, also relies on clinical judgment. Specified in the *Diagnostic and Statistical Manual of Mental Disorders*, fourth edition (*DSM-IV*), this

diagnosis must be made by a physician. Children diagnosed with ADHD frequently seek educational services under the IDEA category other health impaired (OHI) or through Section V of the Vocational and Rehabilitation Act.

In the EMR and EBD categories, Black and, in some states, Native American students have been notably overrepresented. That is, their proportion in these categories is much higher than their proportion in the school system as a whole. While the LD category does not show evidence of over-representation of any group generally, there are some states in which Hispanics or Native American students tend to be overrepresented. The National Academy of Sciences (Donovan & Cross, 2002), which was commissioned to study ethnic disproportionality in special education, explained the difference between these "judgment" categories and the categories that are biologically verifiable:

> The historical concept of a student with a disability or of a gifted student suggests that the characteristics of concern are within the child—an individual or fixed-trait model of ability—and that the student with a disability or a gift is qualitatively different from peers. However, for the high incidence disabilities with which we are concerned, as well as for giftedness, both of these propositions are called into question. . . .
>
> In terms of cognitive and behavioral competence, students fall along a continuum. . . . [T]here is no black and white distinction between those who have disabilities or gifts and those who do not. At the far ends of the continuum there is little dispute about a child's need for something different. . . . But as one moves away from the extremes, where the line should be drawn between students who do and do not require special supports is unclear. . . .
>
> Perhaps of greater concern, however, are *factors that affect where a student falls along the continuum.* For students having difficulty in school who do not have a medically diagnosed disability, key aspects of the context of schooling itself, including administrative, curricular/instructional, and interpersonal factors, may contribute to their identification as having a disability and may contribute to the disproportionately high or low placements of minorities. (pp. 25–27; emphasis added)

Another concern is that the designation of a disability label is stigmatizing, whether it applies to cognitive or behavioral functioning. One of our main points in this book is that special supports should be available to all who need them without the criterion of disability.

This casebook builds on the central finding of our companion book. We quote that statement below:

> To conclude that the children we saw being placed in special education were sufficiently deficient in cognitive and/or social/behavioral skills to warrant

special education placement would require consistent evidence of their failure to progress despite appropriate and adequate instruction in supportive educational environments. This was by no means the case. We found a great deal of evidence of inappropriate and inadequate instruction and school-based decision making that increased the likelihood of special education placement for some children. In many cases, there was simply no way of knowing how children would have fared in more effective educational circumstances or with intensive instructional supports in the regular classroom. In many cases, also, the lack of standard criteria for referral to special education allowed schools to respond inappropriately to the pressure of local norms and high stakes testing. We conclude that it cannot be assumed that high special education placement rates reflect genuine learning and behavioral deficits. (Harry & Klingner, 2006, pp. 181–182)

The case studies illustrate the social processes by which the disabilities EMR, EBD, and LD are constructed. Across these three categories, the social nature of decisions regarding referral, assessment, and placement was evident in our data. While each category presented its own specific problems, numerous external pressures and personal belief systems exerted powerful influences on assessment and placement outcomes in all categories. The arbitrary nature of these outcomes demonstrated the ambiguities and dilemmas of professionals faced with a requirement to convert a continuum into categorical "disability" sets. In all cases, the data also raise the question of whether children had experienced adequate opportunity to learn. We outline these issues briefly in relation to each phase of the placement process.

REFERRAL DECISIONS

We did not see any clear pattern of referrals according to types of schools. In fact, variability seemed to be the hallmark of the referral process. For academic referrals, much depended on the norms of the peer group, the bar seeming to be raised in some of the higher-performing schools. In terms of behavior, children whose behavior was intolerable in one classroom could behave very well in another teacher's room, and conversely, children whose behavior was fine with one teacher were seen as very disruptive as soon as that teacher was out of sight. In classrooms where there was a great deal of misbehavior, decisions about who would be referred seemed to be a toss-up, and it was hard to tell why the teacher selected the students she did for referral. In rooms where behavior was generally good, much milder misbehaviors could gain enough attention to warrant a referral.

With regard to referral rates, although schools showed different patterns of high or low rates, within every school there were teachers who were obviously "high referrers" and some who were "low referrers." School patterns seemed to be a result of the administration's philosophy, but individual rates were very much a matter of teachers' beliefs regarding whether special education was beneficial. There were teachers who annually referred as many as one third of their class; one teacher did this even in a year when her class size was cut by a third. At the most positive end of the high-referring spectrum were teachers who used the child study team (CST) as a means of engaging parent participation and supporting children. At the extreme opposite end were teachers who rarely, if ever, referred children. Some of these expressed the belief that the children were better off in general education with good instruction, while others were reputed not to refer because it required "too much paperwork."

ASSESSMENT DECISIONS

In terms of the psychological evaluation itself, we found just as much subjectivity and variability as in the referral process. Our data indicated that although the vast majority of school personnel viewed the psychological assessment as the scientific aspect that made the process objective, it was really not a discrete or scientific component. Rather, it was influenced by prior events, external pressures, and personal beliefs and biases, played out in a series of human interactions. At the center of this process was the psychologist, a person of extensive training but with his or her own preconceived beliefs, who was compelled to respond to numerous pressures. These included the needs of the child; the needs of the teachers and administrators; the demands of parents; and numerous external factors such as high-stakes testing, the school's reputation in the district, and the demand for timely resolution of the presenting problems.

Overall, we found the arbitrary and social nature of the assessment process very disturbing. It is not that we believe that such assessment could be done without due attention to contextual issues; indeed, we consider this to be an essential part of the judgment. However, we believe that an informed subjectivity would take full account of a child's entire context, rather than being a response to the administrative and social needs of school personnel and school structures.

PLACEMENT DECISIONS

We were particularly concerned about two aspects of decision making regarding special education placements. Our first concern was the apparently unilateral nature of the decision, with practically no input from parents. Even though IDEA stipulates that parents and others on the IEP team should be involved in making placement decisions, most such decisions seem to have been made prior to the placement conference. This practice was typified by one psychologist's description: "We [the psychologist and placement specialist] discuss it prior to the meeting just to make sure we are providing the best for the child. And once we have a unified front for the parents, we can bring them in just so they know what is going on." This unilateral approach was evident in the routine and rapid monotone in which conference coordinators would read parental rights and procedures to parents. There was no opening for questions or discussion, despite the fact that the statements were marked by legalistic and educational jargon that many parents would not have understood.

Our second concern was with the lack of attention to the law's requirement for the least restrictive environment (LRE). This was particularly noticeable in decisions about children designated as having EBD and EMR. For these students, the most common placement was in a self-contained class, often in another school, since not all schools offered programs for these disabilities. Of the four case study students who were placed in EBD programs, two remained in these placements through middle school, one remained for at least 3 years (until the end of our project) with no indication of exit, and the fourth exited special education upon entering middle school. This low rate of exit occurred despite the fact that the three children who remained in EBD self-contained classes consistently met high levels of compliance with the behavioral programs in place in their classrooms. The three children who were placed in self-contained programs for EMR also remained there, it being obvious that there would be no consideration of exit.

In summary, we invite our readers to bear in mind the power of social forces in the placement of minority students in special education. At every phase of the process, children's identity is being constructed in ways that will have long-lasting effects. Our task should be to assist children in building the most positive identity possible. We challenge you to apply this principle to your consideration of the cases reported in this book.

CHAPTER 2

The "Judgment" Categories: Dilemmas of Definition, Assessment, and Placement

Throughout this chapter, it is important to remember the National Academy of Sciences statement that children's cognitive and behavioral achievement falls on a continuum. Decisions about the "judgment" categories really represent professionals' perceptions about how close a child's performance is to an arbitrary dividing line between "normalcy" and "disability." Once we set up such borders, it is inevitable that some children will seem to "fall between the cracks" and that we will sometimes have to decide which of two or more types of difficulties is the predominant one affecting a child's learning.

CONSTRUCTING EDUCABLE MENTAL RETARDATION: CRACKS AND REDUNDANCIES

The EMR category has historically been the source of most controversy regarding ethnic disproportionality. Because of much nationwide objection to the disproportionately high placements of Black children in this category, it is used much less frequently than in the past. For example, while the numbers in the LD category have increased almost sixfold over the past 2 decades, the rates of placement for all ethnicities in EMR have been reduced by almost half. Nevertheless, among those students who are designated EMR, Blacks are more than twice as likely as students of other ethnicities to be identified in this category (Donovan & Cross, 2002). In the school district we studied, the pattern of small numbers but of disproportionate placement of Black students was very evident. This means that while the actual numbers seem acceptable, the fact of Black disproportionality is still problematic.

Dilemmas of Definition

The "educable" mental retardation label has been viewed as representing a "judgment" category, because it relies on clinical judgment as opposed to proof of biological abnormalities. In the early years after the 1954 *Brown* decision, there were numerous charges of EMR programs being used as an alternative to racial segregation, and the *Larry P. v. Riles* case represented the culmination of such concerns.

The definition of mental retardation has remained relatively stable since the inception of the Education for All Handicapped Children's Act (EHA) in 1975, despite several revisions. The 10th definition by the American Association on Mental Retardation (AAMR, 2002) states that:

Mental Retardation is a disability characterized by significant limitations both in intellectual functioning and in adaptive behavior as expressed in conceptual, social, and practical adaptive skills. This disability originates before age 18.

Guidelines for applying the definition require that assessors consider whether limitations in present functioning might be related to cultural and community contexts or cultural and linguistic diversity, while also attending to identifying individual strengths and needed supports.

Many aspects of this definition and implementation guideline are subject to interpretation. A central point of contention has been the IQ cut-off point used to determine what is meant by "significantly subaverage" intellectual functioning. Up until this time, the concept of intellectual ability has been measured by the use of a score on a test of intelligence quotient (IQ). Prior to 1969, the AAMR used a cut-off score of 1 standard deviation from the mean of 100, which meant a score of 85 on an IQ test. In 1969, the AAMR changed the cut-off point to 2 standard deviations from the mean—roughly IQ 70. By this stroke of the pen, many who had previously been determined to be retarded were "cured"! This fact shows what we mean by the "social construction" of disability—that societies decide their own meanings of "disability." Since that change, many states have used a variable guideline of 70–75 on an IQ score. This, however, has only compounded the charge that the process is subjective and ambiguous, since a leeway of just 5 points actually results in large differences in the percentage of students who will qualify (MacMillan & Reschly, 1996).

Dilemmas of Assessment

The actual process of assessing a child on an IQ test is fraught with challenges. Questions arise about which tests are most valid and which are most appropriate to different cultural groups. Since most IQ tests include both verbal and visual/performance tasks, a central issue has been whether the verbal sections discriminate against children with different language or dialect backgrounds or those who have had limited exposure to the language norms in the tests. Consequently, some psychologists prefer tests that are less verbally loaded. Even with less verbal content, some cross-cultural research has shown that individuals' ways of thinking, their ways, for example, of categorizing items, can differ according to their cultural practices and that children who are familiar with the materials in a test will likely do better than those who have not previously used those materials (e.g., Serpell, Mariga, & Harvey, 1993). Another issue is whether children may respond differently to different examiners.

Another dilemma in assessment of EMR is the requirement for a test of adaptive functioning. This dimension is required in an attempt to gain a more holistic view of the child by verifying that his or her delays are general rather than limited to academic achievement. However, the testing is controversial for several reasons: (a) the domains tested are very different from those for which the child is usually referred; (b) scales differ in regard to which domains are emphasized; (c) it is debated whether information should be gathered through observation or the report of a third party; (d) there is no agreement on what cut-off points should be used on the adaptive scales; and (e) the norms for children's adaptive functioning depend on the social norms of their community, which may be quite different from the mainstream norms.

Dilemmas of Placement

In what kind of classroom should children with EMR be placed? IDEA requires that students with disabilities receive a free appropriate public education (FAPE) in the LRE. Although inclusion and mainstreaming are not federal mandates, the requirements for the LRE reflect a judgment that social benefits are important in determining educational benefit for students with disabilities, including MR.

The Twenty-sixth Annual Report to Congress on the Implementation of the Individuals with Disabilities Act (Office of Special Education Programs, 2004) reported that, on average across the states, in the fall of 2002, 49% of students ages 6–21 received special education outside the regular class less than 21% of the school day. However, 58% of students with MR received special education outside the regular classroom. Generally, this shows that students with MR tend to be educated in less inclusive settings, in which they are separated from their nondisabled peers in the quality and quantity of educational opportunities that promote real-world, normalization experiences. There continues to be a tendency to believe that these students can only receive an appropriate education in separate, restrictive environments. The curriculum in these settings seems to perpetuate the thinking that these students can only learn a curriculum that focuses on functional skills and community living.

Another aspect of restrictiveness is seen in suspension and expulsion rates. In the state of Florida, in the period 2001–2002, 1,081 students served in MR programs were suspended or expelled for 10 days in a school year. This number is the largest from any state during that period.

As we mentioned before, the arbitrary dividing line between "normal" and "retarded" means that some struggling learners will not be found to be eligible for special education services under the category EMR. These children may actually receive no special services at all.

CONSTRUCTING LEARNING DISABILITIES: REDUNDANCIES AND DISCREPANCIES

The LD category was originally based on the concept of "unexpected underachievement." This concept indicated an important distinction between children with EMR, who demonstrate overall low developmental and academic achievement levels, and those who are underachieving in school despite being capable of general cognitive and developmental tasks typical for their age. Since evidence of intelligence in the normal range was the centerpiece of this concept, the most common approach to identifying an LD was to compare a child's IQ score to his or her score on a standardized test of academic achievement. A significant discrepancy between measured intelligence and achievement would be considered evidence of an LD.

The LD category has become increasingly problematic because of its intense proliferation. Donovan and Cross (2002) noted that in the 4 decades since its introduction, LD identification rates have increased almost sixfold. While all ethnic groups have been represented in this increase, there has been no significant overrepresentation of Black or Hispanic students, nationwide, but American Indian/Alaskan Native students have been represented at 1.2 times the rate for Whites. It is important to note, however, that, as in all three high-incidence categories, placement rates vary widely from state to state. The "epidemic" rate of increase is of concern to all in the field and it is commonly believed that the category has become a "catchall" for underachieving students. Particularly worrying for English-language learners (ELLs) is the fact that inadequate understanding of the processes of second-language learning might result in inappropriate diagnoses of LD.

Dilemmas of Definition and Assessment

Our research was conducted during a period of increasing widespread uncertainty and controversy among scholars and policy makers about what the criteria should be for qualifying students as having LD. Since then, the reauthorization of IDEA (2004) acknowledged the need to revise both definitions and treatments of this disability, and recommended that consideration be given to use of the approach known as response to intervention (RTI) as a plausible alternative to the traditional criterion of a discrepancy between IQ and achievement scores. In this approach (Vaughn & Fuchs, 2003) the goal is to identify children with difficulties early on and provide them with increasingly intense and individualized instruction to determine whether they will "respond" to these interventions. This instruction is usually described as proceeding in "tiers," and those children who do not respond are likely to be referred for assessment.

"Specific learning disability" was first defined by Congress when it was included as a special education category in the Education for All Handicapped Children Act, or PL 94-142:

> "Specific learning disability" means a disorder in one or more of the basic psychological processes involved in understanding or in using language, spoken or written, which may manifest itself in an imperfect ability to listen, think, speak, read, write, spell, or to do mathematical calculations. The term includes such conditions as perceptual handicaps, brain injury, minimal brain dysfunction, dyslexia, and developmental aphasia. The term does not include children who have learning problems which are primarily the result of visual, hearing, or motor handicaps, of mental retardation, or emotional disturbance, or of environmental, cultural, or economic disadvantage. (U.S. Office of Education, 1977, p. 65083)

The wording of the federal definition is conceptual rather than descriptive, and it does not specify recognizable characteristics or definite criteria for identification. As a result, there has been much ambiguity and widespread variability in interpretation by state and local education agencies. For example, the term "basic psychological processes" is not defined in the federal regulations and only 27% of the states specify criteria for identifying a processing disorder (Mercer, King-Sears, & Mercer, 1990). Yet it was, for many years, a fundamental concept in defining LD. Professional groups have attempted to resolve the issue by proposing alternative definitions, but none has successfully eliminated the ambiguity or included widely accepted, specific criteria. Most states rely on three general criteria for identification of individuals with LD, as specified in the federal guidelines that accompany the federal law (U.S. Office of Education, 1977). However, it is important to note that state and local education agencies have the responsibility to operationalize these guidelines:

1. A significant discrepancy between intellectual ability and academic performance in at least one area of academic functioning listed in the definition.
2. Documented need for services based on achievement below what would be expected for the child's age, grade level, or both.
3. Evidence that the LD is not primarily the result of visual, hearing, or motor handicaps; mental retardation; emotional disturbance; or environmental, cultural, or economic disadvantage.

The first and third of these criteria have generated considerable controversy, which relates more to under- than overidentification. First, it is now widely recognized that the discrepancy model has proved to be a "wait to fail" model, since it is often not until about age 9 that a child's reading delay will be sufficiently behind the chronological age expectation to qualify him or her for the required discrepancy (Donovan & Cross, 2002). This often results in undue delay in implementing appropriate educational interventions. Second, the exclusionary clause seeks to distinguish between inherent disability and lack of opportunity, but can also result in underidentification of students from economically disadvantaged backgrounds, thus providing one more reason for delaying appropriate interventions. Worse, the failure to meet LD criteria might mean greater likelihood of low-achieving students from minority groups being placed in EMR programs. We note, also, that the delay in implementing instructional interventions is tied to the requirement that a child must "qualify" for special education services. As mentioned above, these difficulties have been addressed by the IDEA (PL 108-446, 2004) allowance for alternative approaches to LD identification.

Despite all this debate in the field, the professionals in the schools in which we carried out our research did not seem to view the eligibility criteria as ambiguous. They knew what the criteria were and that there should be a discrepancy between intellectual potential and achievement as well as a processing deficit. Yet they also seemed to feel quite comfortable with applying these criteria arbitrarily. Our data indicate that psychologists who, for whatever reason, believed that the child should be placed would then make decisions that would allow them to manipulate the child's classification in a way that would get the child special education services. One method was simply to ignore the fact that the discrepancy had not been met, as with Paul, a Hispanic kindergartner who was referred for emotional and behavioral difficulties was but determined by his psychologist to have LD even though his achievement test scores were actually higher than his IQ score. Another approach was to choose an IQ measure on which the child could score higher in order to show a 15-point discrepancy between IQ and achievement. One psychologist told us that she had been told that "I try too hard to place the child by using different instruments." She added, "But this is because I think the child really needs help!" Another option is to choose an instrument known to be less verbally loaded, so as to give the minority child an opportunity to be assessed more on nonverbal performance than on language.

Dilemmas of Placement

The LRE is also a concern for students labeled LD. While the general trend is for these students to be educated in the general education classroom, there is considerable variation across states (U.S. Department of Education, 2004). Nationally, in the fall of 2002, more than half of these students in the elementary school grades spent less than 21% of the school day outside the regular class. In the state of Florida, however, less than half of these students (42.81%) spent less than 21% of the school day outside the regular class. Issues also arise regarding optimum class size for part-time LD placements. If instruction is to be truly individualized, what should the ratio of student to teacher be?

CONSTRUCTING EMOTIONAL/BEHAVIORAL DISORDERS: DISCREPANCIES AND DISTURBANCES

Across all ethnicities, the overall rate of placement in EBD is considered lower than theoretical estimates would expect, resulting in the view that students are actually underidentified in this category (Donovan & Cross, 2002). Nevertheless, EBD is a problematic category for two reasons: First, there has been a steady increase in EBD placement numbers for all ethnic groups over the past two decades, the rate of increase being highest for Black students (Donovan & Cross, 2002). Second, among those children who are found eligible for EBD, the placement rate is one and a half times higher for Black students than for White. Specifically, the risk of EBD classification for Black students is approximately 1.5%, while the rate for White and Native American students is approximately 1.0%, and much lower for Hispanic and Asian students. In states where numbers of Native American students are large, however, EBD placement is notably high (U.S. Department of Education,

1999). These trends must be seen as problematic because of the stigma attached to this label, the high rate of dropout, and the restrictiveness that generally characterizes EBD placements.

As the cases in this book illustrate, the ambiguity and overlapping of the categories EBD, ADHD, and LD rendered the diagnostic process close to meaningless. The technical term for the interactive nature of these categories is *comorbidity*, but we will refrain from using this terminology because we believe that it contributes to the impression that the children truly have intrinsic deficits that interact. In the cases we studied, we were seldom able to see this as a reasonable interpretation.

Dilemmas of Definition

As with all three high-incidence categories, definitional issues are of central concern to the concept of EBD. The federal definition used by IDEA has not changed substantially since the introduction of the Education of All Handicapped Children's Act (EHA) in 1975. This definition identifies five dimensions of maladaptive behavior as the criteria for a diagnosis of EBD and requires that at least one be identified as adversely affecting a student's academic performance across "a long period of time" and to a "marked degree" (PL 108-446, 2004):

1. Inability to learn that cannot be explained by intellectual, sensory, or health factors
2. Inability to build or maintain satisfactory relationships with peers or teachers
3. Inappropriate types of behavior or feelings under normal circumstances
4. General pervasive mood of unhappiness or depression
5. Tendency to develop physical symptoms or fears associated with school problems.

The federal definition also excludes students labeled as socially maladjusted (SM), but there is no operational definition to distinguish between SM and EBD, and the typical presenting behaviors are similar across both categories. These concerns, along with the lack of specificity regarding how to interpret the "long period of time" and "marked degree" clauses, have led to much controversy in the field. Clearly, perceptions of what constitutes a "long period of time' and "a marked degree" will vary according to the expectations and tolerance of the referring teacher and the behaviors normative in the child's peer group. Thus the act of referral itself depends on teacher perception. Our data revealed tremendous variability across teachers and across schools regarding the types of behaviors and the extent of severity that would be likely to result in a referral.

Dilemmas of Assessment

Once a child is referred for evaluation, the assessment procedures for EBD typically involve one or more standardized achievement tests; an IQ measure; rating scales of behavioral severity and frequency; and, in some states, projective testing. Although it has been noted that the use of projective testing varies by region (Hosp & Reschly, 2002), in the school district we studied projective tests are considered an essential component of assessment for EBD. Our research revealed the most common of these to be the House-Tree-Person, the Kinetic Family Drawing, Roberts Apperception Test, and Sentence Completion Test. The choice of tests, however, depended on the psychologist, and we learned that some used only a few or even partial aspects of tests, while others routinely administered the entire battery. Our data indicated numerous sources of subjective, even biased, interpretations of these projective instruments, and one observation in particular confirmed these tests' potential for extremely subjective interpretations.

Another aspect of the assessment is the law's requirement that the behavior must be adversely affecting the child's academic performance. Thus, the question arises of whether the primary concern is the child's learning difficulties or his or her behavior. Clearly, this dilemma is another source of subjectivity, since the chicken-egg argument cannot be empirically resolved and it is left to the judgment of the assessor to decide which label will predominate. Our data underscored the difficulties of this dilemma. Three of our case study students who were ultimately labeled LD had initially been referred for behavior problems. One of these children, Germaine, was not at all behind in his academic work and showed no evidence of LD and little evidence, if any, of EBD. Conversely, one of our case study students, Edith, who was labeled EBD, had been referred for poor academic performance, with only a mild reference to behavior as an issue. Collateral information, in which the child was reported to have threatened to kill herself, led the psychologist to evaluate her for EBD and to label and place her accordingly. As we will detail in this case, the child was experiencing extreme frustration in response to severe teasing by her peers. This information was not taken into account in the evaluation.

As in the case of LD, and despite the high-profile debate in the field regarding the definitional and assessment issues related to the EBD category, school personnel in the school district we studied appeared unaware of these controversies. With rare exceptions, personnel at all levels expressed confidence in the ability of the psychological assessment to determine who should and who should not qualify for EBD services. Some personnel did point to the issue of interaction between EBD and LD, but the overall assessment of the process was positive and largely unquestioning.

Dilemmas of Placement

The law's requirement for the LRE is one of the greatest concerns in placement decisions for students labeled EBD. In the school district under study, children so labeled were most typically placed in self-contained classrooms, often in a school other than their neighborhood school. Research on the rates of restrictiveness in EBD placements indicate that this is one of the main areas of disproportionality for Black students. *The Twenty-second Annual Report to Congress* (U.S. Department of Education, 2000) revealed that while 52.9% of White students with EBD spent less than 21% of the day in separate placements, only 35.3% Black students met this criterion.

These restrictive placements resulted in several limitations and increased isolation for the children. First, the fact of being bused was most often accompanied by a different schedule from their general education peers, including breakfast, lunch, and dismissal times. Second, it was clear that the EBD separate class placement brought with it a stigma of bad behavior that led school personnel to raise the bar in terms of expectations for the labeled child. Third, while we did observe one very good EBD program, others were excessively restrictive and relied almost totally on "boot-camp" style behavior management techniques. These techniques not only were unpleasant and excessive, but also seemed unlikely to result in children learning self-monitoring behaviors and skills. Moreover, instruction in these programs did little to provide students with access to the general education curriculum.

SUMMARY

These case studies illustrate an array of issues that contribute to the ethnic disproportionality in special education. Because of the law's requirement for signs of intrinsic deficit as criteria for services, school personnel often engage in a search for such deficit without taking into account the numerous contradictions and discrepancies in the construct of disability. Moreover, the focus on intrinsic deficit tends to trump issues of context, resulting in a search that excludes serious consideration of the many risks inherent in schooling itself. As you read these cases, we urge you to reverse this emphasis, seeking contextual clues first and intrinsic deficit last.

PART II

Case Studies

CHAPTER 3

Emotional/Behavior Disorder or Attention Deficit Hyperactivity Disorder?

Robert: *"I'm a gangsta, tha's why!"*

It was mid-June, just a week or so before the end of the school year, and we were observing for the second time in Ms. Gonzalez's first-grade classroom in South Park Elementary School, located in one of the poorest neighborhoods in the city. In a conversation the week before, Ms. Gonzalez had described this class as the "second worst" she had encountered in her 10 or more years of teaching in this inner-city school. The school served a majority of African American children but there was a growing population of Hispanic students. Ms. Gonzalez's first-grade class was predominantly African American and she had described the children's family situations as marked by extreme poverty and very little adult attention. She described the children's difficulties as being mainly "cultural," remarking that many came to school with "absolutely no social skills, not knowing how to walk, sit in a chair . . ."

A FIRST GLIMPSE OF ROBERT—FIRST GRADE

We arrived late to Ms. Gonzalez's class and there were about 25 children seated on the floor area in front of her desk, ready for story time. After about 5 minutes, there was some rustling at the door as if someone was trying to come in. It seemed the door was locked. Our field notes read:

> A minute later, a door at the back of the room opened and two boys slipped in with a mischievous expression on their faces and sat down surreptitiously at the back of the group. . . . The teacher frowned and said, "Oh, so you're back." She warned them in a very stern voice to

behave properly and went on reading the story. But the two boys increased their attention-seeking behavior, such as lying down on the floor with their legs in the air. Ms. Gonzalez . . . told one of them to come over to the side of the group near to her. He got up and went . . . and within a moment, he started talking to a child in front of him. All these behaviors were done in a deliberate manner, accompanied by the boys' covert giggles and smirks. Ms. Gonzalez's facial expression and strident tone suggested that she was quite angry.

This was our introduction to Robert and his friend, Tyrese.

MS. ROBINSON'S SECOND-GRADE CLASS

In September, Ms. Gonzalez greeted us with a big smile, saying that she was really happy that she had been given an ESOL (English for speakers of other languages) class, which meant she had half Hispanic and half African American children, and the Hispanic kids were "calmer and better behaved." She took us to meet Ms. Robinson, a Black veteran teacher of about 32 years, in whose class Robert and Tyrese were now placed. Ms. Robinson's colorfully manicured nails flashed as she waved her hands and narrowed her eyes, openly expressing her disdain for these two "terrible" boys. That day's observation in this classroom was the first of about 12 observations during that school year.

This second-grade class was described as the "low" group, about 15 of the 36 children being repeaters. A district reorganization that year had provided this needy school with extra funds, which the principal used to cut by half the ratio of students to teachers. Because of space limitations, the new ratio was accomplished by assigning two teachers to all classes, usually pairing a newer teacher with one who was more experienced. In Robert's classroom, Ms. Robinson's partner was Ms. Lopez, a young Hispanic woman, recently graduated from college.

The two teachers were very different. Ms. Robinson wore a stern expression, sometimes bored, sometimes angry, and reserved most of her instruction for reprimands and disciplinary threats. During many of our observations, she would leave the room and not return for 15 minutes or more. When she was present, the children were generally quiet, though not necessarily on task. Ms. Lopez always greeted us with a big smile, but her manner with the children ranged from gentle and friendly to frustrated and angry. It seemed that her job was mainly to lead the lessons, which, she explained, were based on a great deal of "routine" so that the children would know what to expect.

We did note that the instruction offered by Ms. Lopez relied almost totally on routines and that her own level of English was weak in pronunciation, vocabulary, and grammar. In terms of grammar, for example, she would frequently use structures such as "he does goes" or "he show you." Additionally, we noted instances where she seemed not to be able to assist the children in enriching their vocabulary. For example, when asked to suggest an adjective that described a classroom, a child said, "Has lots of things in it." Ms. Lopez hesitated, saying, "Yes, but . . ." then trailed off, instead of offering the child alternative adjectives such as *full* or *crowded*.

Meanwhile, the discipline offered by Ms. Robinson was generally harsh, even unkind. The following excerpt was not an extreme example of her manner:

> While Ms. Robinson is at the back of the room two of the students in the front pass gas. Ms. Robinson calls out, reprimanding them. . . . She says in a disgusted voice, "I don't have patience for this mess. You think you're gonna come in here and upset this classroom? Don't even try that!" She then comments on the "junk" they must be eating at home and says, "Someone needs to go home and tell their mamma they need a laxative tonight." Then she tells a student to open the door.

Ms. Robinson's discipline, however, was sporadic. On one occasion, she held a conference at her desk with a parent, in tones loud enough to be heard across the room. Ms. Lopez, trying to conduct the lesson, became increasingly rattled, as Robert, Tyrese, and others wandered around aimlessly, chatting to their friends. Every now and then Ms. Robinson would look up and reprimand the class sharply, then return to her conversation with the mother. As the chatter rose again, Ms. Robinson exclaimed to Jose, "I"ll take you to the cafeteria to your momma. That'll stop that smiling!"

ROBERT'S REFERRAL

Despite Robert's reputation as "terrible," our observations that fall showed his behavior to be very variable. On some days he was quiet—either on task or dreamy. On other days, he was out of his seat and generally wandering around the room, though not particularly disruptive. Ms. Lopez expressed the opinion that Robert's problem was mainly related to whether he had taken his medication. She also stated that his friend, Tyrese, was a bad influence and that he "followed Robert around" and often got him into trouble. In

December, Ms. Robinson reported that Tyrese had been referred "for his behavior." Robert had not been referred, although he was now "more off the
wall than ever" because he didn't seem to be taking his medication regularly.

In the first week after the Christmas break, we were told that there had
been "a big problem" with Robert and Tyrese. Both boys had been suspended
and Robert had now been referred for evaluation for behavioral issues. We
never learned what "problem" had occurred. Ms. Robinson told us that
Robert's mother had come to a Child Study Team (CST) meeting and had
given permission for an evaluation. However, after the suspension was over,
the principal placed both boys on half-day attendance. Tyrese's mother,
objecting to this arrangement, withdrew him from the school, saying she
would have him placed elsewhere. Robert's mother agreed to come to the
school and pick him up at 11:00 every morning. When we asked the school
counselor about this arrangement, she replied:

> His behavior is so bad we just can't keep him all day. The mother's
> attitude is, "Don't call me, he's your problem." So we told her,
> "Well, you'll have to come pick him up at 11:00." That way, it's her
> problem.

The counselor said that this arrangement would continue until Robert was
tested, which she expected to occur soon, since he was "the most urgent" of
all the students referred.

Robert's half-day placement did continue until he was tested. Some
5 months later, in May, his mother told the principal she would no longer be
coming to pick up Robert at 11:00 and that they needed to go forward with
the evaluation for which she had signed consent in January. Robert was re-
instated on a full-day basis and was evaluated by the psychologist in June.
At that time, Ms. Robinson complained that she had suddenly been asked to
write anecdotal reports on his behavior. Ms. Lopez added that, although
Robert's achievement was at the "pre-primer" level, he would be promoted
to the second grade because his name had not been put on the retention list
in January and it was now too late to retain him.

By the time Robert was assessed, his behavior had deteriorated notice-
ably and the teachers frequently put him to stand at the front of the room.
In May, soon after his return to full-time placement, our notes describe an
incident where, in Ms. Robinson's absence, Ms. Lopez was standing behind
the screen at the back of the room talking on her cell phone for about
10 minutes. During this time, as our notes describe, Robert was "in constant
movement, kneeling, standing . . . always on the move . . . stands at the front
swinging his arms." Emerging from behind the screen, Ms. Lopez hurried

towards him, exclaiming, "No! Not at my desk!" Our final observation of
him in his second-grade classroom read:

> Robert is standing toward the front of the room. He is hopping up
> and down with his shoes off [all the children have their shoes off to
> be weighed and measured for some reason]. Then he puts them on
> and is quiet for a few minutes. Then he starts rocking from side to
> side, hops, jumps, walks over to stand in line. He looks over at me
> and grins. . . . Soon after this, Robert is doing flips on the floor
> and crawls under a desk. The line of standing children blocks the
> teachers' view of him.

ADHD OR EBD? PART-TIME
OR SELF-CONTAINED PLACEMENT?

At the placement conference early in the fall, the entire placement team expressed dismay and amazement that the psychologist had found Robert not
eligible for a placement in a program for children with EBD. Robert's assessment report stated that his intellectual functioning was well below average,
but that his challenging behaviors were related to ADHD, along with a lag in
academic skills. His emotional condition was not found to be in any way un-
usual, nor did he display any signs of disturbed thought processes. Emphasizing that Robert's impulsive responses were typical of a child with ADHD, the
psychologist required that a physician be consulted regarding this possible
diagnosis. In keeping with the low IQ score, Robert's low achievement was
attributed to limited cognitive ability. The psychologist recommended that
Robert receive special education services under the category of other health
impaired (OHI). He would receive these services for reading and math, within
a special education classroom serving children with a range of high-incidence
disabilities. He would spend the rest of the day in general education classes.

Despite the notation of his behavioral difficulties, Robert's IEP contained
only academic goals and recommendations to the teacher regarding strategies such as prompts to stay on task, frequent praise and encouragement,
academic tasks at his skill level, part-time small-group setting, and weekly
progress reports to his parents. There was no reference to any systematic plan
for modification of his behavior.

Our observations of Robert during the fall in the special education classroom noted a supportive atmosphere provided by a young Black woman who
worked enthusiastically with between 6 and 10 children. There seemed to
be little difficulty with him in this classroom, but in the general education

classroom, where there were two teachers to about 30 children, the teachers reported that everything depended on whether Robert had taken his medication. Our observations showed that his behavior was indeed variable; some days he was quiet and compliant and other days he did everything he could to provoke the teachers. However, we also noticed that there seemed to be little individualized attention paid to the level of his academic tasks. As he worked on the computer, we noted the following:

> His approach to the computer comprehension task is to guess by looking at the picture, looking at the four choices of word, and picking one that looks like it should go with the picture. Often he's correct. But he also seems to be using memory, because when I ask if he guessed he says, "No, I did this yesterday." For several items I make him read the entire passage and he definitely cannot read many of the words. I prompt him and then he understands readily and can choose the correct word. He has no trouble with listening comprehension, but he just can't read at this level. When I tell Mr. Paredes [the teacher] about my observations, he expresses surprise, saying that the program should be set to Robert's level.

By December, several of our observations of Robert in both his general and special education settings showed him to be increasingly aggressive toward his peers. He would quickly become angry if someone sat in his seat, or he would insult them for no apparent reason. One day, after observing several displays of this type of behavior, the researcher asked him why he was behaving like this. He replied, "I'm a gangsta, tha's why!"

Robert's part-time special education placement lasted until March that academic year. One day, on arriving at the school, we were told that Robert had been suspended for 10 days for "threatening to kill a teacher." We were not able to get any more details than this statement. In a matter of days, the psychologist had met with Robert and, in his words, "updated his evaluation." Robert was now found to be eligible for services for children with EBD and was moved to another school.

We will not go into depth regarding our findings of Robert's final special education placement. We refer interested readers to consult the follow-up study by Hart (2003).

JACINTHA: ROBERT NEEDS HELP

Beginning with the period of Robert's half-day placement, and until his removal from South Park Elementary, we came to know his mother quite well.

During five visits to their home and numerous telephone conversations, we learned that Jacintha had nine children, because, she said, "I just love having children." During the summer vacation, we met two of the four older children, who lived with their paternal grandparents in a nearby state. We learned that Jacintha was so well organized that even her 4-year-old knew where to find her pen. We learned that she had a large collection of children's books obtained from Goodwill. We observed her affectionate interactions with her children as Robert lay across her lap gazing up into her face as she talked, while the other children clustered around, joining spontaneously into our conversation. We learned that she lived in a tiny, poorly maintained rented apartment in the heart of the inner city. We learned also that she had once had a problem with doing drugs but now was "clean." Most of this information was gleaned in our first visit to Jacintha's home and was reinforced during all our subsequent visits.

Jacintha participated consistently in all school conferences and responded immediately to calls from the school. In Robert's CST and placement conferences, she was polite, even deferential, to the team members, yet it was evident that her keen attention missed nothing that was said. Despite her full participation, there were team members who frequently spoke of this mother in a derogatory manner. We offer here only one such example; there were many more.

At the first placement meeting, Jacintha arrived late because she had been in the school office discussing a problem that was occurring with Robert's younger brother, who was in kindergarten. Jacintha was very worried about this child's behavior. The assistant principal, who was new that year and had not been involved in the previous year's decisions, expressed to us great concern about the extended half-day placement that had occurred, stating that it was close to "malpractice." Nevertheless, he seemed to expect little of Robert's mother, stating that she had "five children here and four farmed out somewhere else." As they waited for Jacintha to arrive, several team members expressed the opinion that she would not show up. Making no attempt to disguise his negative expectations of her, the assistant principal told the group in a sarcastic tone that it was ironic that she says she is deeply concerned about her son's behavior yet does not show up at the meeting. He rolled his eyes, shook his head, and sighed as he expressed the opinion that Jacintha would not be bringing the anecdotal reports that he had shown her how to write. Later in the meeting, when he asked Jacintha if she had done the anecdotals, she replied quickly, "Yes, sir, I have," handing over a brown envelope.

We cite, below, our notes on the concluding conversation at that meeting, to indicate both this mother's intense concern and the acknowledgment by some team members that the school had not done well by Robert:

Before the meeting ends, Jacintha gets everyone's attention by starting to talk and lightly tapping her hand on the table as she speaks. She plainly states that she wants to make certain that the school follows through with their plan because last year Robert was sent home from school every day at 11:00 and that did not help him. The psychologist tells her in a soft and reassuring tone that the school did contribute to the problems and they will "certainly" help to fix them. She smiles at him and says quietly, "You might as well start on my younger son now."

Questions

1. Review the definitions for ADHD and for EBD. Do you feel that Robert has either of these disabilities? Why or why not? Consider the concept of "opportunity to learn" in Robert's case.

2. Once Robert had threatened to kill a teacher, his label quickly changed. This also changed his placement. In your opinion, should the type of label a child receives dictate services?

3. Research the definition of the term *manifest determination* and what IDEA states about discipline regarding this concept. How does this apply to Robert? Pretend you are an administrator at South Park Elementary. Based on the law, what types of disciplinary procedures might you have ordered for Robert?

4. The teachers in this case reported that Robert was much better behaved when he took his medication. Seek information on the use of such medication for children with ADHD. Develop and discuss with your group your views about children and medication.

5. Robert's second-grade classroom observations reveal a lack of consistent disciplinary practices. Think about your own style of discipline. Write a personal reflection about the style of discipline that you find to be most effective when dealing with student behaviors.

6. The issue of racial and social-class stereotyping is very common in schools. How do you think school personnel's views of Robert's family affected their decision making? For a closer look at Robert's and other case study children's families, read the article by Harry, Klingner, and Hart (2005), cited in the reference list.

CHAPTER 4

Emotional/Behavior Disorder
or Gifted?

Kanita: *"There's nothing wrong with her, she just wants her momma"*
(Kanita's grandmother)

Kanita was 6 years old and in the first grade when we first saw her. It was March of the school year and this was our first classroom observation in Centerville Elementary School, located in the heart of a historically African American neighborhood. This school had the second-highest rate of special education placement among the 12 schools in our study. The school's programs included resource room instruction for students with LD and self-contained classrooms for children designated as EMR. Students qualifying for services in a program for EBD would be moved to another school.

FIRST GRADE AT CENTERVILLE

Kanita's black eyes shone as she turned defiantly to her teacher and refused to stop what she was doing on the computer. Apparently, this was not her scheduled time. It was difficult for us, as observers, to tell what was scheduled, since very few children in the room seemed to be doing anything constructive. The following excerpt from our field notes illustrates the climate of the classroom:

> The teacher begins a lesson on synonyms. Her voice is loud as she
> tries to talk over the noise in the class. . . . Soon after she asks a
> question, students at the computer request help and other distractions
> occur so that she is not focusing on any one thing. She then walks out
> of the classroom for something and when she returns she asks
> another question about synonyms. There is little student involvement.
> Some are looking at what their classmates are doing at the computer.

At least one student is cutting paper, while others look aimlessly around the room. . . . The boy sitting next to me keeps talking to Kanita, who is at the computer. Someone tells the teacher that Kanita is doing Math Corner on the computer and the teacher tells her not to. Kanita replies that she is going to do it anyway. A child near me tells his neighbor to behave and says, pointing to me: "She writin' down what you do." The neighbor looks around and replies, "She ain't writin' 'bout me, she writin' 'bout her!" [pointing to the teacher]. A child at his table starts singing Aretha Franklin's "Respect."

We conducted a lengthy interview with the teacher, Ms. Edison, a White woman, who told us that this was the second-worst class she had had in her 16 years of teaching. Stating that she used to refer only a few children each year, for the past 3 years she had referred "more than half the class." She felt that the parents of children in this neighborhood had become increasingly mistrustful and defensive over the years and that only about half of them would respond to invitations to come and discuss their children's problems. Ms. Edison described her classroom management style as "very relaxed," but she believed that the children "knew her limits" and she would become stern when she had to. She stated:

> Their behavior got worse in the year because they couldn't do the academics . . . because at the beginning of the year the behavior doesn't start off that bad. . . . I do know they get more comfortable with me as they get to know me and they know what they can get away with and what they can't . . . but I think if they were competent doing their class work they wouldn't sit there being a clown or trying to kick someone under the table.

Kanita was referred by Ms. Edison that spring and was promoted to the second grade in the fall, with an evaluation pending. Her second-grade teacher, Ms. Taylor, was a youthful Black woman whose cheerful but stern approach evoked a generally positive response from her students. At the placement conference in September, Ms. Taylor reported that Kanita had started off troublesome but seemed to be settling down.

EMOTIONALLY DISTURBED

Kanita's referral record focused totally on her behavior, using the district's required checklist of behaviors as well as an "anecdotal" report. On the checklist, the teacher scored Kanita as "often" or "excessively" having difficulty with "attending behaviors" (does not complete tasks, short attention span, easily distracted), "disruptive behaviors" (temper tantrums, crying, moody), "interpersonal behaviors" (dominating others, physically aggressive, threatening teachers/students with bodily harm"), and "self concept."

The anecdotal reports were written on a form that had four columns: "date," "antecedent events," "observed behaviors," and "consequences." These reports comprised records of Kanita's behaviors during the 7 days immediately preceding the official referral. For the first 3 days the behaviors noted were similar to those in our observation, such as "walking around, saying rude things, taking kids' pencils; stood outside door; walked out of reading class then came back in." However, on the 4th to the 7th days the noted behaviors became more severe, progressing from "tried to bite, kick, and slap at the teacher"; "stuck a student with a sharp pencil"; "attempted to throw a chair at a child." In the earlier entries, the "consequences" column listed the teacher "talking to Kanita" about her behavior. For the three attempted physical attacks, the consequences were "wrote up a case management form, called home, and requested parent conference."

Kanita was evaluated for special education about 3 weeks after the beginning of the next school year. When the two researchers arrived to observe the evaluation, the psychologist, Ms. Lewis, a pleasant, White woman probably over 60, greeted us amicably and advised us to sit quietly at a table in the back. Mentioning to us that the teacher's referral was based on Kanita's challenging classroom behaviors, Ms. Lewis commented that the family was "dysfunctional," Kanita being raised by her grandmother because her mother was incarcerated and her father was not involved.

Seated about 6 feet behind the table at which Ms. Lewis and Kanita sat, we were able to hear and record all the conversation in detail. We observed the first two parts of the evaluation—the IQ test and a set of projective tests. The third part, the academic testing, was done on another day. Kanita cooperated eagerly and consistently throughout the 2 hours it took to administer the Wechsler Intelligence Scales for Children-Third Edition (WISC III). She persisted on puzzles that she found difficult, and after a 10-minute break for a fire drill, she settled down to the next task without hesitation. When this test was complete, Ms. Wilson gave Kanita a short break, after which she conducted the projective testing.

Kanita began the projective testing with great enthusiasm, complying with Ms. Wilson's request to draw a house, then a tree, then a person. Next, when asked to draw her family, Kanita willingly drew what seemed to be about five figures. The psychologist asked her to name the people in the picture and Kanita began cheerfully. As Ms. Wilson's questions became increasingly personal, including a line of questioning about where a male cousin slept, Kanita began to respond with some reluctance. At one point, Kanita disclosed that her mother had been in a "program . . . after she came out of jail." As Ms. Wilson pursued this for more information, Kanita's reluctance became increasingly evident.

Our notes on the evaluation were very detailed, including virtually every question and answer, much more than we could report here. Also, since we are not trained in interpreting projective testing, we do not think it appropriate to engage in a review of the process we observed. Suffice it to say that Kanita's discomfort, which began with the personal family questions, became increasingly obvious throughout the series of tests. These included sentence completion tasks and the Roberts Apperception Test, a set of pictures about which Kanita was required to construct a story. Some of the pictures were suggestive of intra- or interpersonal conflicts, such as one with a boy holding a chair over his head as if about to smash it onto the floor, and one in which two Black boys seem to be confronting a White boy, whose face wears an expression of alarm. By the end of the battery of tests, Kanita had slid halfway under the table and was mumbling many of her answers.

At the end of the projective testing, Kanita left for lunch and Ms. Wilson commented to us that Kanita's reluctance on the projectives indicated that she was "denying her feelings." When we asked if Kanita's reluctance could be in response to embarrassment about her mother's situation, she said no, because children in this neighborhood are so accustomed to family members being incarcerated that they are quite "blasé" about it. Ms. Wilson went on to reiterate her earlier belief that the family was "dysfunctional" and that there were a "bunch of people living in the home."

A couple of days later, Ms. Lewis reported to us that Kanita had been very uncooperative during the Woodcock-Johnson testing, trying to skip pages and refusing to complete math problems unless the examiner pointed to them directly. The results of the entire assessment were as follows:

IQ: WISC III: Verbal = 111; Performance = 102; Full scale = 107
Freedom from distractibility subscale = 118
Woodcock Johnson: all scores between middle to high first grade, except applied problems, which was 2.6

Kanita was found to qualify for a program for students with EBD. The evaluation report stated that Kanita was cooperative throughout testing on the IQ scale, but that during the projectives, she withdrew verbally and "attempted to shut down." The report also said that Kanita was in denial of her feelings and that her Roberts Apperception stories revealed a great preoccupation with violence. The reason given for the placement recommendation was that, because of poor anger and impulse control, Kanita needed a structured class with behavior management to ensure success.

The placement conference was attended by Mrs. Smith (Kanita's paternal grandmother) and one of Kanita's aunts (Mrs. Smith's daughter). When the psychologist reported her findings, the grandmother commented quietly but firmly, "She's a bit rebellious. But there's nothing wrong with her. She just wants her momma." The aunt did believe that Kanita's behavior was troublesome and believed that Mrs. Smith was too soft on Kanita because Mrs. Smith was sorry for Kanita's not having her mother. Both agreed to the placement, which was at a different school, to which Kanita would be bused.

In reviewing Kanita's history, we noted that her kindergarten records were very different from those written by the first-grade teacher who referred her. In the kindergarten reports, all items had a check mark or plus, indicating "attained" or "working on skill," with no marks indicating unacceptable behavior. When we spoke with Ms. Little, the kindergarten teacher, a Black woman with a reputation as an excellent teacher who seldom referred children, she said that Kanita had been quite emotional during her kindergarten year, would cry easily, and had a tendency to temper tantrums. Ms. Little had not found these behaviors very problematic and told us that she was able to redirect Kanita or calm her down with quiet warnings before Kanita's temper escalated. Ms. Little said that she believed that these behaviors were caused by the child's missing her mother. She said she was shocked when Kanita's behaviors escalated to such an extent as to "put the school in an uproar" in Kanita's first-grade year. She had never expected that Kanita would earn the label EBD.

SPECIAL EDUCATION:
"DO YOU KNOW WHY SHE'S HERE?"

We visited Kanita in early October, a couple of weeks after the start of her placement in the self-contained EBD program at a nearby school, which also served predominantly African American children. Upon arrival at the classroom, we were greeted by the teacher, Ms. Thorpe, a White woman with a cheerful countenance and a firm classroom manner. As we introduced ourselves, she said, "So, do you know this child? Do you know why she's here?" Ms. Thorpe said that Kanita had been well behaved since her 1st day in the class, was working well, and was obviously very bright. As in all the EBD classrooms we observed, the program was based on children earning behavioral points throughout the day in order to earn privileges. There were about 12 children in the class. Our observations of Kanita in this classroom revealed a totally different child from the one described in her first-grade behavioral reports. For example:

Second-grade EBD class (March)
Ms. Thorpe talks about the how ocean plants need oxygen. . . . She says that even fish need oxygen and they come up to the surface to take in air. As she says this, Kanita puts her lips up briefly, imitating how a fish would suck in air. She is totally engaged in the lesson.

Second grade, PE, general education (March)
We spot Kanita standing in line with her mainstream group. She is waiting patiently for her turn, and when it comes, she runs enthusiastically through the course, ending with a big grin. She returns to her group.

Throughout Kanita's second-grade year, this teacher's reports and our observations of Kanita were all positive. In the spring of second grade, the teacher's summary note at the IEP review meeting was "Kanita loves to learn and is eager to please." At this point, Kanita's file contained daily reports signed every day by her grandmother since her placement in the EBD class. For the list of behaviors noted, more than half were summarized as A and all the rest were B. Ms. Thorpe described Kanita as unique among her peers in her ability to work independently. She did not see her as having a disability. Looking over Kanita's files with us, Ms. Thorpe exclaimed that it was hard to believe all the things Kanita used to do at Centerville Elementary.

THIRD GRADE: MAINSTREAMED

At the beginning of the third grade, though still based in the EBD program, Kanita was mainstreamed for reading and math. Her revised IEP stated that she needed "a low teacher student ratio and needs to be supervised during most activities." Kanita did very well that fall in her mainstreamed placement, and the following January she was fully mainstreamed. On one occasion, as our researcher left the classroom after talking with Kanita, a boy chimed in eagerly, "Kanita always gets A's!" Kanita smiled and looked down shyly. The following is an example of Kanita in her general education class that year:

Third-grade general education, math class (February)
They are going over a graph that has pictures of vegetables plotted at different points. . . . Kanita raises her hand for every question and when she does not get picked she mutters the correct answer under her breath. . . . Ms. Watson then hands out a worksheet with a grid

and they must identify the items. . . . Kanita finishes very quickly and has them all right. She is the first to complete both sides of the worksheet. Most of the kids raise their hands for help. Ms. Watson sends Kanita and another girl to the computers for math because they are finished. . . . After Kanita is through, Ms. Watson tells her to go to her table and write her multiplication tables from 1 through 9. In a short space of time she has 1 through 4 completed.

In the spring of Kanita's third grade, she took the state standardized tests. Her report stated: "State Comparisons: Reading—middle third; Math—highest third. National Comparisons: Math problem solving—98th percentile; Reading comprehension—78th percentile."

FOURTH GRADE: GIFTED

In the fourth grade, Kanita was fully mainstreamed all year and was also placed in a part-time gifted program back at Centerville, her old school. Despite expressions of doubt by administrators at Centerville that Kanita would succeed in this program, she excelled. Our observation in that classroom showed her participating eagerly and actually being the first to solve a science-based "treasure hunt" game organized by the teacher. The teacher asked us if we thought that perhaps Kanita had been "misplaced" in the EBD program.

Kanita did better in the gifted program than in the general education fourth-grade class, where she was occasionally reported back to her EBD teacher for behaviors such as passing notes or talking out of turn. While it seemed that the bar had been raised for her behavior, the EBD teacher, Ms. Thorpe, felt that this was in Kanita's best interest. She saw Kanita as having great potential and wanted to be sure she got the best possible opportunities. She was very protective of her, resisting any attempts to release her from the IEP, because, she said, she "didn't want to see her back in the [EBD] class next year."

In her fourth-grade year, also, Kanita's annual IEP review meeting revealed that she seemed to be having more difficulty, related to her wish to live with her mother. Her grandmother, her father, and his fiancée were present and reported that Kanita now spent weekends with her mother and would cry because she wanted to be with her all the time. Another concern was Kanita's shyness with adults. Her IEP goals included "express her needs in an assertive manner," "maintain eye contact with adults and respond," and "recognize her own moods and verbalize her feelings." Because of these concerns, Kanita received weekly counseling.

"A BUNCH OF PEOPLE IN THE HOME"

Throughout the 3 years of our research project, we visited Kanita's home four times, but it only took the first visit to learn that Kanita was treasured by this family. However, she was not the only treasure. The living room of the small house was filled with photographs of aunts, uncles, cousins, "grands" and "great-grands," as well as trophies and certificates earned by the children, at least three of which were Kanita's. On that first visit, Mrs. Smith brought out an album stuffed to the brim with Kanita's school reports, notes home, Mother's Day and Valentine cards, and any school information pertaining to Kanita from her Head Start days to the present. We learned that one of Mrs. Smith's daughters and her child also lived in the home and that several cousins came directly to their grandmother's house after school every day, where they stayed until their parents came to pick them up in the evening. We learned also that Kanita's father lived nearby and, like his four siblings, was a frequent visitor to his mother's home. There were, indeed, "a bunch of people" in and out of the home.

Kanita's grandmother, although she disagreed with the diagnosis, was very pleased with the success Kanita experienced in her EBD program. She felt that the teacher really cared about Kanita, and on one occasion, when Kanita was sent back to her EBD class because of passing notes in class, Mrs. Smith told us that she was satisfied with the decision because Kanita tended to take advantage of soft teachers.

We end Kanita's story here. Those who wish to know about her fifth-grade year must read a separate account, by Hart (2003), who pursued Kanita's case to the end of the child's special education placement. We will reveal, however, that Kanita finally exited the special education program upon entering the sixth grade, at middle school.

Questions

1. Review the current definition of EBD. What do you believe to be the causes of Kanita's problems at school during her first-grade year? Do you consider Kanita to be a student with EBD? Examine the details of her behavior referral records.
2. Why do you think Kanita's behavior seemed to be better in her gifted class? Research national, state, and district definitions of giftedness. What is the nature of the curriculum in these programs? What are the rates of placement of minority children nationally?
3. Kanita spent 4 years with the label EBD even though her first EBD teacher wondered why she had such a label. What is your view of the teacher's

decision to keep Kanita on an IEP in order to protect her? Make a list of the pros and cons of placing such a label on a student.

4. School personnel referred to Kanita's family as dysfunctional. Develop your own definition of what constitutes a "functional family." Read the article in the reference list by Harry, Klingner, and Hart (2005). Do you consider these to be functional or dysfunctional families? Why?

5. Even with the movement toward more inclusive schools, students with behavior disorders tend to be the last group included. Go online and research the national percentages for inclusion of all students with disabilities. How does this compare to the percentages for inclusion of students with behavior disorders? Check the same for your state and local district (if available).

CHAPTER 5

Emotional/Behavior Disorder, Learning Disability, or Just Sensitive?

Germaine: *"Why you looking at me?"*

I can qualify Germaine for LD. . . . His reading was OK but his math was very low. His verbal IQ was low. He doesn't really have LD, but with this [special education] teacher, he'll get the nurturing and individual attention he needs. (Psychologist's comment)

Germaine was an African American boy attending Centerville Elementary School, which served a low-income population in a historically African American neighborhood. Although we conducted between 8 and 12 observations in Germaine's second-grade classroom between late fall and spring of that academic year, we did not notice him particularly during the course of those observations. In fact, when we heard of his referral in the spring, we were surprised that we were not aware of him or his difficulties.

We discovered that Germaine had been retained in the first grade and had been evaluated for special education midway through his repeat year. He was found not eligible for special education services at that time.

REFERRED AGAIN: BUT BY WHOM AND WHY?

In April of his second-grade year, Germaine was referred once again for evaluation. It was not clear from the record, or from our conversation with the teacher, who had initiated the referral. We were not sure if this was part of the administration's new policy of initiating referrals rather than relying on teachers to refer. We were told that a parent conference had been called to consider retention again for Germaine, but the outcome of the conference was to refer for evaluation. We assumed that this decision was made in view of the school district's ruling that a child could not be retained twice.

We first heard of the referral in May, when we saw Ms. Taylor, Germaine's upbeat Black teacher, writing anecdotal reports for Germaine. She had written notes almost every day from May 1 through May 19, as follows: In the column for "antecedents" she wrote "normal condition" for each date. In the column for "behavior," she wrote: "Smiles to self; looking at pencil; talking to self; playing with pencil; writing on desk; fingers in mouth; sitting on feet in chair; looking at worksheet with hands on head." Under "consequences," she wrote: "Direct student to task; frowns; does not complete work; teacher asks, do you understand what you're doing? He replies, no."

Ms. Taylor told us that she wondered if the child might be "hearing voices or something" because sometimes he seemed to "have tics," just looking around, playing with his pencil. When asked if his facial expression changed as he did these things, she said no, "he just gazes around." She commented that she knew the child's mother was in a "mental institution." She went on to say that she was "told to do anecdotals on him." Shrugging, she looked at the paper and said she really didn't know what else to write. She added that she was told to "just keep writing."

The psychologist's comments on Germaine's referral were equally vague. Remarking that he had been evaluated previously and found ineligible, this time "they" were telling her that there definitely had to be "something wrong." She said she agreed to test him but only if they furnished her with "ironclad anecdotals." She did not recall the details of the child's previous evaluation, beyond the fact that "the home situation was part of it."

The referral was also supported by behavioral checklists filled out by Ms. Taylor, the homeroom teacher; and Ms. Cooke, a White, veteran second-grade teacher. Of a total of 50 items across four domains, the teachers' selections included difficulties with attending, interpersonal skills, and self-concept, but the actual items chosen differed greatly. Ms. Taylor checked only 8 of the 50 as excessive items and Ms. Cooke checked 19.

EVALUATED AGAIN

Germaine was evaluated by a White female psychologist perhaps in her 60s. Her finding regarding Germaine's emotional condition was unequivocal: "Germaine continues to be an emotionally healthy child." Nor did she find any evidence of attention disorder. Rather, the report stated, over a 2-day period of testing, Germaine attempted all the tasks, seemed to be motivated, and never tried to stop or avoid the testing. Further, the report noted that he approached his tasks "very methodically and handled his frustration very adequately, maintained good eye contact, and sat still." Specifying that his responses to the projective testing were generally "happy and upbeat" and indicated a solid sense of right and wrong, the report concentrated on Germaine's academic needs.

Tested on the WISC III, Germaine's overall IQ score remained at 83, as in the previous testing. However, instead of his verbal and performance scores remaining evenly balanced, his performance score rose to 93 and his verbal score fell to 76. Based on this information, as well as the fact that in his previous evaluation his expressive-language score was 29 points below that of his receptive language, the psychologist concluded that Germaine was finding increasing difficulty in expressing himself. Stating that the performance score represented the most accurate measure of his intellectual functioning, she instructed that this score be recorded for purposes of comparisons with other test scores. When interpreted in this way, Germaine's scores did reflect a discrepancy between his IQ score and his achievement levels, especially in math. This made him eligible for special education services under the category learning disabled.

Germaine's academic levels ranged widely. At the high end, he scored at a 3.3-level in writing samples; within the second-grade range on letter-word, passage comprehension, and calculation; and within the first-grade range for applied problems and dictation. The report concluded that he was having "great difficulty in math; can't regroup; poor money concepts."

The psychologist noted one contradiction within Germaine's performance in the testing. According to the report, although Germaine scored low on several verbal items, later in the evaluation he used some of the words that he claimed not to know. Our observation notes specified some of these; for example, when asked what the weather was like in a picture, Germaine replied quickly, "Summer." Earlier, in response to a question about the four seasons, he had failed to propose the word *summer*, even with some helpful prompting from the assessor. Most striking to us was the sudden increase in Germaine's vocabulary when he began making up stories based on a set of pictures, an activity in which he engaged with great enthusiasm. His statements included, "He don't have no children. He childless"; "She tried to escape into the house and the police came and they arrested the thief. . . . He choked her and she got unconscious"; "The suspect . . . the police search for him with helicopters and canines and they catch him and put him in jail for life."

The outcome of the recommendation was that Germaine should be placed in a program with a smaller teacher-pupil ratio and an IEP. Deficits in language should be addressed daily, and he should receive small-group counseling.

SPECIAL EDUCATION: PRIMARY OR INTERMEDIATE?

We began observing Germaine in October that year. In all, we conducted 12 classroom observations, which included his two special education classrooms, his general education homeroom, and one observation in a music class. We also interviewed both his special education teachers and his father.

Germaine had three special education teachers throughout his third-grade year. Ms. Perez, the primary special education teacher to whom he had been assigned, was a young Hispanic woman who ran a structured classroom in a gentle manner that supported the psychologist's description of her as "nurturing." Within a month, however, Ms. Perez found it necessary to send Germaine to the intermediate special education class for reading because his reading was "fluent" and "on grade level." That class served fourth and fifth graders who had an IEP for reading and was taught by Ms. Merriweather, a young White woman whose excellent rapport with her class resulted in a flexible but constructive learning atmosphere. However, she resigned late in the fall and was replaced by Ms. Church, a young Black woman who was a recent college graduate.

Ms. Perez was baffled by Germaine's having an IEP for reading. She suggested several reasons. Perhaps, she surmised, in writing he didn't "want to be bothered to write a long sentence," a problem common to most of her students. Or, perhaps, she said, he may have been "fighting in class" and falling behind in his work. Finally, she mused that it was probably his "attitude . . . processing problems. . . . He needs to verbalize more. He will not tell you what he feels. . . . But you know the story, don't you? [At home,] that's hard for him."

In math, Ms. Perez described Germaine as taking a long time with his work because he was very unsure of himself. Her approach was to allow him to do a smaller number of sums than other students, emphasizing correctness rather than quantity. She reported that his skills were progressing—he was doing addition of three digits with regrouping, which was third-grade level. His subtraction with regrouping of three digits was weaker but he did grasp the borrowing steps. She stated that upon his mastering the three-digit subtraction with regrouping, he would be on grade level.

Reading was the big puzzle. The intermediate special education teacher, Ms. Merriweather, reported that Germaine, reading at a 3.1 level, was actually ahead of all her students. Most were at least one grade below, some more than that.

"WHY YOU LOOKING AT ME?"

Germaine's behavior in class seemed to vary with the context. Ms. Merriweather, the intermediate special education teacher, described him as "daydreamy," tending to "zone out." Even in the middle of writing something, he might just stop and daydream. She stated that he was never disruptive, but he would always report someone else who was. Ms. Perez, in contrast, did not find Germaine "daydreamy" or "zoning out," but she was concerned that he would get very upset if any of his peers bothered him at all. She said he was also slow with his work because he was "too busy complaining and minding other people's business." He had low self-esteem and would always think others were saying something bad about him. He would exclaim, "Why you looking at me?" Ms. Perez would encourage him to be positive by saying that maybe his peers were admiring something he was doing. Our observations did note Germaine pouting and becoming very irritated if someone took his pencil or seemed to be teasing him.

As the year progressed it became evident that Germaine was very sensitive to classroom context, but we also saw that he was capable of staying on task in circumstances that were quite distracting. However, he could also join in with a misbehaving group of peers. In his primary special education class, Ms. Perez's strong instruction and gentle but firm management seemed to bring out the best in him. The same was true in his initial placement in Ms. Merriweather's intermediate special education program. When she left the position in the middle of the school year, however, a number of unfortunate events occurred.

First, it took a month or more to find a replacement for Ms. Merriweather. During that time, all the special education students were sent to the primary program and Ms. Perez found herself, along with a paraprofessional, responsible for 42 students in an age range from kindergarten through fifth grade. Like many of his peers, Germaine became very unsettled during that period. Yet in the midst of considerable classroom uproar, we noted Germaine talking quietly to a peer—no worse than the rest of class. However, Ms. Perez said that he was frequently "whiny and complaining," talking a lot and tending to be rather aggressive, getting into arguments, or would "just sit there" when he didn't understand something.

The other unfortunate result of this staff change was that the replacing teacher, Ms. Church, had great difficulty establishing and maintaining classroom control. In February, the class, which in the fall had consisted of about 16 students, now had 24, whom the teacher divided into four groups, by level. In one of our observations in February, we noted that there were 31 students in the classroom.

Through our four observations in Ms. Church's classroom, the atmosphere was chaotic. There was always excessive loud talking among the students. Sometimes the class would begin quietly but the arrival of the fifth graders would convert the situation into an uproar. Germaine would sometimes cooperate with the teacher's attempts at instruction, but at other times, he would join in the talking and laughing. We never saw him engage in any disruptive behavior, even on a day when a fight broke out in the class and security had to be called. In April, after two months of this atmosphere, Ms. Church informed us that an administrative decision had been made to "split" her class, taking the fifth graders out.

Germaine's general education third-grade classroom was also characterized by a great deal of chatter. Classroom management consisted mainly of exhortations by the teacher, Ms. Harris, urging the children to "be quiet, be quiet!" In our observations we never saw Germaine create or get into mischief. On one occasion we saw him become very upset when a girl took his assignment and refused to give it back. Glaring at her, he gestured with his hand that he'd like to sock her in the face.

Perhaps because of this atmosphere, or maybe because of stereotypical expectations based on Germaine's special education placement, this general education teacher did not seem very aware of Germaine's skills. In a science lesson, Ms. Harris told our researcher that she knew that he "probably could not do the work, but she would make him do it anyway and not give a grade." However, as the lesson progressed, the teacher asked Germaine to read a passage and he did so quickly and accurately. The passage included words such as *dinosaur* and *fossils*. With a surprised expression, the teacher gently tapped his head and said, "Boy, you're trying to fool everyone around here!" Germaine smiled.

There was one occasion when we saw that Germaine could behave just as badly as his peers. This was in a music class, taught by a White woman in whose class we had seen normally well-behaved kindergartners run wild. In this case, as Germaine's third-grade classmates chased into the room, shouting and running, Germaine jumped on top of a chair and started running on top of the row of chairs, laughing loudly. Soon he was playing catch with another boy while other children argued, cursed one another, banged on the piano keys, and walked out of the room as they wished. From this class, we followed Germaine back to his primary special education class, where he sat quietly and got quickly to work.

"MOST IMPROVED"

At the end of Germaine's third-grade year, Ms. Perez told us she was "very pleased" with his progress and she would describe him at the "most improved" in her class. As we spoke, Ms. Perez went over Germaine's scores on the reading portion of the Woodcock Johnson (WJ). As she came to his name, she exclaimed: "OK! Germaine! Look at that! All math calculation, 4.5, so this is telling you fourth grade!" Ms. Perez had not tested Germaine on the reading portion of the WJ, explaining that the intermediate special education teacher would do that. However, she was confident that he would be scoring toward the end of the third grade.

Regarding behavior, Ms. Perez saw Germaine's difficulties as being primarily social: "He needs to be away from the kids in order for him to work." She added that it was "hard for him to know behaviors if they are good or bad." However, as we pressed for more detail, Ms. Perez's answers seemed to point more to Germaine's competitiveness, his unwillingness to wait his turn to offer an answer. She summarized:

> I tell him, "If you know the answer that is fine, but you don't have to give the answer all of the time!" I think he wants people to know that he knows all of the answers, he always has to be perfect.

Germaine was to be promoted to the fourth grade, continuing to receive special education services.

In our last conversation with Ms. Perez, she spoke of the importance of trying to get her students ready for the statewide testing. Even though, at that time, the scores of students in special education were not counted in the assessment of schools, Ms. Perez's students did as well as many in general education, and she felt a responsibility to prepare them for the testing. This underlined an issue we knew to be of great concern in this and all the schools in our study: The competition for improved grades in the state's standardized testing. In this school, as in some others, we had been explicitly told both by administrators and teachers that there was a great "push" to get special education placement for all those children "who needed it" before their year to take the state testing. This meant careful monitoring of children at the lowest academic rungs, in order to have them evaluated for possible special education eligibility.

GERMAINE'S FATHER

An interview with Germaine's father made it clear that this child had full and individualized support at home. His mother's psychological difficulties, it seemed, had resulted in her being away from the home for long periods, and in his father's opinion, Germaine was missing his mother and demanding more attention as a result. The father described his son as very competitive. He was concerned that Germaine should be doing better both academically and behaviorally and appreciated the school's efforts to individualize his educational program. He felt that the special education placement was a good solution because of the small class sizes and individualized attention. When we met this father, unexpectedly, some years later, he said that he believed that Germaine had improved a great deal because of the placement and he was satisfied with the school's efforts.

Questions

1. In your opinion, why was the school so eager to try to qualify Germaine for special education services?

2. Review the current definition of *specific learning disabilities*. What do you believe to be the causes of Germaine's difficulties? Do you consider Germaine to be a student with a disability?

3. Review the No Child Left Behind Act (available online) to find out what current policy is on standardized testing for students with disabilities. Do you believe that students with disabilities should take the same tests as their nondisabled peers? Do you think their scores should count in the evaluation of the school?

4. What effect, if any, do you believe that class size has on a student's ability to learn? Contact a school in your local district and find out what the average class size is for elementary school classes and special education classes. See if you can find research on the effects of class size.

5. It seems that the psychologist interpreted Germaine's scores in such a way as to allow him to "qualify" for special education services. She believed that the placement with a strong, nurturing teacher would be to his benefit. Do you think this was achieved? Do you believe that the ends justified the means?

CHAPTER 6

Emotional/Behavior Disorder or Learning Disability?

Matthew and Austin: *"I have a dream . . ."*

I have a dream that there will be no more wars. There will be no more fighting, throw away the drugs. I have a dream that one day there will be no more rich people poor people. We will all be equal. I have a dream that we will all wear helmets with our stoooters [*sic*] and bikes. (Matthew's composition: Martin Luther King Jr.'s birthday)

Sunnybrook Elementary School was located* in an upper-middle-class suburban neighborhood. The student population at Sunnybrook represented, according to the principal, "one of the few primarily Anglo pockets left in [the] county" (55% White, 23% Hispanic, and 17% Black). Among the students, 18% received free or reduced-price lunch in contrast to the other schools in our study, which ranged from 65%–99%. Three percent of the students in the school received English for Speakers of Other Languages (ESOL) services. In the 2 years in which we followed the placement of students from general to special education at this school, all the referrals made in the classrooms we observed were of Black students who were bused to Sunnybrook from "across the highway" following court-ordered desegregation.

STANDING OUT?

The first time we entered Ms. Jones's general education classroom, two students stood out from the rest. They were the only two Black males in a class of 35 and they were both seated at desks isolated from the rest of their classmates, who were seated in neat rows. One of the boys, Austin, was much

*Authors' note: This chapter was written by Elizabeth Cramer and Keith M. Sturges.

46

larger than the rest of the students and the other, Matthew, much smaller. When we asked Ms. Jones, a Black second-grade teacher with several years' experience, for a list of potential students whom we might be interested in observing as target students, it was no surprise that Austin and Matthew's names were at the top of the list.

Emotional and Behavioral Issues

The two boys were very different from each other in their behavior. Unlike Austin, who was constantly seated at the teacher's desk, Matthew was isolated in the back of the classroom and had one-on-one attention from a classroom assistant whenever she was present. Matthew was not an instigator of trouble, and he was obviously very sensitive. When teased or frustrated, he tended to withdraw or, in the teacher's words, "shut down" and "freeze on the spot and refuse to move." He would do this in the classroom, or, more troubling to the teacher, in the hallways when his class was supposed to be moving along to the next activity. His teacher also reported that he would occasionally have "violent rage days" when his anger would be out of control, and she reported one incident when he stuck another student with a pencil. She felt that he had a great deal of repressed anger. She attributed his emotional problems to circumstances in the home and a need for attention at school that he was not receiving at home.

Austin demanded attention, seeming to use his personality to cover insecurities about his work. Field notes indicated that whenever he paid attention and understood what was happening, he worked well, but he could be quite disruptive: Behaviors noted in various observations included "contradicted the teacher, called out comments during tests, rolled and moved around in his seat, crawled on the floor, refused to respond to the teacher." Austin also had a very difficult family situation, which was thought by his teachers to be a contributing factor to his learning and behavior problems. We did not know whether his parents were involved in Austin's life. He lived with an uncle, who took on the role of primary caregiver and attended his school meetings. We witnessed him attending one meeting dressed as a woman and were told by the school that this was how he normally dressed and that Austin found this embarrassing. During our follow-up work we were informed that his father had recently died.

Matthew was much quieter than Austin, but was generally inattentive, easily distracted, and often out of his seat. The teacher's differentiation of these two children from the rest of the class was evident not only in their seating arrangements but also in the fact that she tended to ignore consistent out-of-seat behavior from Matthew, but not from other members of the class. The teacher described him as a "sad child" with emotional problems, who could not concentrate and needed a smaller class. She was also very patient with Austin's disruptions.

Academic Issues

Matthew and Austin also differed from their peers in terms of their academic levels. Austin's scores varied widely, suggesting that he would do well when he tried and very badly when he did not. Matthew's scores were more consistent but were generally the lowest in the class and he was always behind the rest of the class in completing his work. Of four math test scores posted on the wall, Austin's were 90, 9, 62, and 4, while Matthew's were 70, 74, 72, and 0 (we assumed he did not do the last assignment). Most of the other students consistently scored between 75 and 100. Matthew's insecurity about his skills was evident in his very slow pace of work and his constant erasing and rewriting. However, his reading and math were close to grade level and his writing was neat and his spelling quite good. Nevertheless, Matthew's work stood out as the lowest in his class. Although he consistently tested close to grade level on achievement tests, most students in his second-grade class were actually performing above grade level.

Writing samples of Matthew's work showed much neater, overall better-quality work than Austin's. Most of our samples of Austin's work were of routine rather than creative writing since his work folder was thin because he often left his work unfinished. His handwriting was more uneven than Matthew's; he sometimes mixed upper- and lowercase letters, showing spelling errors but no signs of letter reversals or difficulty forming letters. The writing was easily legible but the sentences were poorly structured as the following science sample shows:

observations of potting soil	observations of school yard soil
I noticed	In the school yard
thaht the potting soil	soil Big Dark Rock
see a litte white thing	
in it	

REFERRAL AND DECISION MAKING: SCIENTIFIC OR ARBITRARY?

By the end of second grade, Ms. Jones referred both boys to special education. Although the original concerns about the boys were similar, the outcomes of their respective evaluations were quite different.

Austin's Evaluation and Placement:
If the Shoe Doesn't Fit, Wear a New Label

When Austin was referred, the referral papers stated: "The major presenting problem is his disordered school behavior, which is described as being severe in degree of psychological disturbance. The presenting problem has occurred over the past several years. Other concurrent issues include his poor academic performance." In the referral report, Ms. Jones characterized Austin as

> distractible, failing to finish assignments, having difficulty maintaining attention, having problems playing quietly, talking excessively, interrupting, and failing to consider safety. He did not complete tasks, had a short attention-span, forgot material presented and was easily distracted, often avoided competitive activities, frequently did not participate in ongoing class activity, frequently appeared frustrated or confused, lacked self-confidence, and needed much teacher praise and encouragement to continue to take part in classroom activities.

Austin was tested for IQ, achievement, cognitive processing, and personality using the Wechsler Intelligence Scale for Children—Third Edition, the Woodcock-Johnson Tests of Achievement—Revised Edition, Bender Visual Motor Gestalt Test, House-Tree-Person, Kinetic Family Drawing, and a student interview. He scored within normal limits in all areas, but with wide variations. His verbal IQ score was in the borderline-low average range (79), while his performance IQ score was average (96). His achievement scores ranged from the mid-70s to the mid-90s. The psychologist noted deficits in reading, writing, and math clusters, which were discrepant from his achievement IQ of 96, but not from his verbal IQ of 79. The assessor's decision to use projective tests indicated that the team expected Austin to be found EBD. However, once the results of the tests were in, the language about Austin's problems was changed to fit his disability. The presentation of evaluation findings read, "Austin was referred for testing in order to assess his poor general academic performance and his difficulty in specific learning areas." This wording fit the label that was the ultimate decision of the multidisciplinary team: LD.

Austin's second-grade teacher was also somewhat contradictory in the opinions she expressed about him. When she was interviewed the following year about Austin, she stated that she knew he had LD and never thought that his problems were emotional. This was contradictory to previous field notes as well as her recommendations at the time of his referral. During the later interview, she acknowledged that emotional problems related to family circumstances contributed to his academic difficulties, and stated that "we were lucky we did manage to get him into our program here." She stated that as long as he was in a class of no more than five children, he would do well academically.

Matthew's Referral and Evaluation: Good-Bye Sunnybrook

During an interview, Ms. Jones, Matthew's second-grade teacher, described Matthew as a sad child with emotional problems, who could not concentrate and needed a smaller class. His evaluation report stated that the reasons given for his referral were difficulty staying in his seat, not completing tasks, short attention span, impulsive and hyperactive behavior, trying to dominate others, threatening others, preferring solitary noncompetitive activities, lacking self-control, demonstrating moods, easily frustrated and confused, lacking self-confidence, demanding attention from teacher and peers, and showing lack of remorse when confronted about his behaviors. The report concluded that academic achievement was average but that he showed "serious learning difficulties." His academic scores were, however, higher than his IQ scores. His IQ was low average, with a verbal score below average at 73, performance score of 93, and a full scale IQ of 81. He scored poorly on measures of social comprehension and showed no signs of depression. He was given the same battery of projective tests as Austin and was found eligible for EBD services in a self-contained class. The psychologist recommended a smaller class with more structure and Matthew was placed into a full-time self-contained class for students with EBD, which was offered at a different school.

Once the boys were placed in their respective special education programs, their educational paths became quite different.

AUSTIN: "WE WERE LUCKY WE DID MANAGE TO GET HIM INTO OUR PROGRAM HERE"

Austin was placed into a part-time varying-exceptionalities class late in his third-grade year. He spent approximately 40% of his time in this class and the rest in his homeroom.

General Education Classroom

His third-grade homeroom teacher, Ms. Goddard, was a Black woman who had grown up in Austin's community. She had originally worked as a paraprofessional in a special education classroom until she earned her degree to become a general education teacher.

Ms. Goddard demonstrated patience for Austin's needs, as was evident in the following example taken from a classroom observation:

> When Ms. Goddard is finished handing out papers, she comes over to go over the lesson with Austin. She reads the question to him and reminds him where he can find the answer in the book. Austin reads silently at his seat tracking words with his pen as he reads. Ms. Goddard comes back over to Austin and asks him what he can tell her about what he read. She asks him what he read about heat and how heat travels. He can't tell her. She asks him about conductors. She asks him to tell her three things he learned and three things he remembered. She stays and works with him one on one to find these answers. She is at his desk leaning over him helping him go through the book. Meanwhile, the rest of the students are working independently.

Both prior to and after his placement in special education, Ms. Goddard took a great interest in Austin and modified instruction in both content and presentation so that he would be able to learn. Ms. Goddard made many comments about her attachment to Austin:

> I want him to feel, not just academically, I'm looking for self-esteem. I want him to have more confidence in himself. Not to be unwilling to take a chance and try and do unfamiliar things. I want to expose him to things that he is not exposed to at home. You know, you have to watch with student-teacher boundaries, but I would love to take him home on weekends to experience the things he doesn't get to experience.

While the other students (more than 30 of them) worked independently on assignments, Ms. Goddard would give Austin one-on-one attention, taking time to be sure he understood what he had to do. During one of our interviews with her, I asked her if she always spent so much time one on one with him. She replied:

> If you ignore Austin, that's where Austin will start to blurt out and you see the behaviors. And he typically will just come to me if he does not get something, you know. "Ms Goddard, I don't get it." . . . You have to hone in on him. . . . That's when you get the behaviors from him if he sits and doesn't know what to do. As long as he has direction and he knows what he is responsible for doing, he is OK.

Austin continued to stand out in the general education classroom. He was the only student who came to class without homework, the only student who was significantly below grade level, and the only student diagnosed with a disability. He was also the only student who came to class with no supplies and had his own box of supplies, provided by Ms. Goddard, which remained in the classroom. His behavior stood out as well, and the students and teacher made allowances for this.

During our observations in the general education classroom, he was always working on assignments. Often, his assigned tasks were different or less demanding than those given to his peers (such as answering fewer questions or drawing instead of writing). The system used to grade his work was also different. Ms Goddard would call on him for answers that she knew he would be able to provide so that he would always be able to participate. If there was something that he did not feel able to do, he would tell her he did not want to answer and she would call on somebody else.

Austin had friends in the class. During our observations of an assembly, he and other boys were drawing faces on their hands and making their "faces" joke around with one another. In the cafeteria, he would run over to friends at other tables laughing and fooling around. But he was also a bully, bossing other kids around, pushing or hitting them as he passed by, and taking things from them. Regardless of these behaviors, the other students all seemed to tolerate his differences and like him as a classmate. He displayed an outgoing personality, and when he knew an answer, he was very eager to participate or to blurt out what he knew.

During two observations of Austin in PE, we noted that he was a key team player, often taking the lead and guiding students on what plays to make. In free play, he chose hockey both times and he was the leader of the team both times in planning players' positions and in scoring. His impulsiveness showed in his volunteering to demonstrate before he knew what the task was. For example, when he realized that he had to show specific square dance steps from the last class, his hand shot down and he started shaking his head to indicate "no" when the coach looked at him.

During a science class, Austin disturbed his entire table, stealing the magnifying glass and rocks that students were supposed to be viewing as a group. He used the glass to look at various items around the classroom, rather than the rocks, and argued with students who were trying to get the materials to use. At one point, Ms. Goddard came over and asked him about what he saw. Then he finally looked at the rocks and got excited about what he had seen. He ran to Ms. Goddard to tell her about it. This example sums up what we saw in all our observations of Austin in the general education class: He would play around off task and act out when he did not understand what he was supposed to do, trying to give the impression that he did not care. Then, with a little one-on-one guidance from the teacher, he would fall in line and become very engaged in the task.

Special Education Classroom

In the special education classroom, although there were far fewer students (the numbers grew as the year went on from 5 to 10), less time was spent with Austin one on one, since all the students in the room needed supervision while working. His special education teacher, Ms. Hanks, was a young, White, mild-mannered first-year teacher. Austin completed less work in this special education classroom than in the general education classroom. He was off task during most of the observations of him in special education. When he did complete work, his answers were mostly wrong. Ms. Hanks took the time to explain things to him, but he seemed uninterested in her explanations.

After Christmas break, his behavior deteriorated in Ms. Hanks's class and he refused to do any work. Ms. Hanks attributed these changes to problems going on in the home and his uncle, who suffered from a terminal illness, getting sicker. Austin would frequently blurt out comments in class and refuse to complete any assignments. Ms. Hanks felt that his calling out and lack of work were distracting to the other students and she was afraid that they were starting to imitate his behaviors, so she moved him to a desk at the back of the room facing away from the rest of the class. This was reminiscent of his time in the general education second-grade classroom prior to his referral. He began to spend the class period with his head down on the desk doing nothing.

Austin told us that he liked Ms. Hanks's class because she was nice and did not make him do too much work. He indicated that he didn't like Ms. Goddard's class because she made him read and work all the time and it was boring. So while he showed a preference for Ms. Hanks and her class, he did no work in that class for the last few months of school and did most of the work in the regular education class. Both teachers attributed the decrease in homework to the fact that his uncle's health was deteriorating and he was the only person who had previously helped Austin with homework.

Counseling

Austin had spoken to the school counselor on several occasions. A Black woman in her 50s, Mrs. Staples believed that family problems were the primary cause of academic and emotional problems in students, and Austin was no exception. She told us that Austin had seen the corpse of another one of his uncles at that uncle's funeral and had become preoccupied with a fear of both death and church. She was concerned that he also had developed a preoccupation with blood and chose to write stories about this when given opportunities for free writing.

Fourth Grade

When we followed up with Austin during fourth grade, we learned that his family life continued to be a stressor that affected his school performance. According to his teachers, his father's death in November that school year sparked an increase in challenging behaviors. He was failing all his classes and receiving zeros for assignments in both the general and special education classes. His general education teacher said that any homework that was turned in was completed by Austin's uncle rather than Austin. In the general education class, he had a teacher whom we had observed in previous years and rated to be an outstanding teacher. He also had moved into the special education class for intermediate students and had a different teacher there. Both these teachers were White females in their 50s with many years of teaching experience. Both reported that Austin seemed angry, depressed, negative, and in need of attention.

MATTHEW: THIRD GRADE SPECIAL EDUCATION

Matthew's placement meeting took place over the summer, and he began at his new school in the summer before third grade. This new school offered a program to which all students labeled with EBD from surrounding schools were bused. The class was entirely self-contained, made up of about 10–12 students, almost all male and all Black. Students from Matthew's class and students from a class of varying exceptionalities ate lunch together, at a different time from their nondisabled peers. A structured behavior modification system was in place in the EBD classes, with levels of freedom earned by the accrual of points. There was a teacher and a paraprofessional. The former, Ms. Appleton, was a White woman perhaps in her fifties and the latter, Ms. Hill, was a Black woman of about the same age.

"Very Organized, Very Regimented"

We first spoke to Ms. Appleton approximately 6 months after he began the EBD program. She told us that Matthew had moved through the point system very quickly and that he was dependable. She said that Matthew was "a sweet child. He came in very stubborn but now he's my little pet." She stated that his behaviors were very good and she would probably exit him the following year. She also said that he was below grade level in reading but on grade level in math. When we questioned her on another day about why he was placed in the EBD program, she then told us that he was functioning on grade level in all subjects but behaviorally he still had some areas to work on. However, when she tried to give me examples of behavioral issues, she reported only one story from when he first came to the school and did not want to eat his lunch. She attributed the changes in his behavior to the consistency in her classroom.

When we questioned her about possibilities for Matthew, she replied:

> Hopefully next year he should be mainstreamed. . . . We're going to try him on a trial mainstream next year. . . . If he can finish up and earn it, which I think he can. He should . . . do well in certain types of classrooms. [Interviewer asks what she means by that.] Very organized, very regimented, very this is the schedule, this is the way we do things. Matthew thrives off of being able to date his paper correctly, put his full name on the paper correctly, put the heading on his paper beautifully! [She takes out work samples to show me how neat his handwriting and headings are. This is not the first time she has shown me this.] I mean, he thrives off of doing those things in such a perfect manner. . . . When there's chaos he also thrives in a negative way. . . . He just can't go, ho hum; he's got one extreme or the other. Middle of the road just does not do it for him.

In another interview with Ms. Appleton, she attributed changes in his behavior to "consistency":

> A lot of consistency. A lot. He thrives on consistency and he also strives off of inconsistency to get out of sequence. If there's a sub in the room, Matthew is the first one to volunteer to set the room off. [Laughs.] The first one to volunteer to do nothing. But if we run everything very consistent, Matthew runs beautifully. Falls into regiment just perfect. The kind of kid you can see going into the military service later. Doing extremely well in the system, in the military, because he knows how to follow regiment and God forbid anything falls out, he's gonna be the one to set everybody off [laughs] and running the opposite way. That's a lot of Matthew's behaviors.

Matthew's Behaviors

Ms. Hill, the paraprofessional, told us that Matthew was above average academically, but "he has a little temper that comes through every now and then." She said that the temper was not "intentional." Coach Peter, the PE teacher, told us that Matthew was well behaved and "did not act out." He said that when yelled at, Matthew tended to isolate himself and cry.

In the classroom observations, Matthew appeared to be well behaved and a hard worker. He was always the student chosen to run errands to the office or to do favors for the teachers. While he played around with his friends in the cafeteria, he never got into fights, as did some of his peers. He was on the highest level behaviorally and usually earned the privilege of being the first to line up.

Once, during a PE observation, Matthew did respond physically to being provoked by a peer. After a student hit him with a ball, the two began pushing and shoving. Matthew removed himself from the situation, and when he returned, he moved to a new spot and started playing a new game. He appeared to have good problem-solving skills and the PE coach confirmed that this is what he did when he had a problem.

Socially, the class comprised boys who were angry at each other one day and best friends the next. Matthew was no exception. There was one boy, Ronald, with whom he consistently seemed to talk and hang out. On one visit, we were told that Matthew had, uncharacteristically, been in several fights with students the day before. When we asked him about the fights, he told us that he was fighting because everyone was trying to fight with him and saying bad things about his family. He indicated that he did not like his classmates very much, but that he still liked school and that he liked his new school better than his old school because he was learning more and the school was nicer.

Instructional Quality

Classroom observations of his EBD placement revealed two important and potentially contradictory factors: Matthew's academic performance had improved greatly; he was working close to grade level and completing his assignments. However, the instruction he was receiving was inferior to that he had received in the general education class. Through six observations of him in his new school, including one full-day observation, we observed several troubling issues.

First, his actual time spent in instructional activities was greatly reduced. The special education students at Leafville Elementary School ate their breakfast in the cafeteria after the school day began, while the general education students were attending class. During one observation of breakfast, our field notes demonstrate wasted time during the school day:

> 8:25: bell rings for students to go to class. . . . Special education classes stay behind in the cafeteria after the day has started. After the students finish eating, Mrs. Hill calls, "Gentlemen.". . . Students get up and move to a bench close to the teachers' table. . . . Boys wait on the

bench, Matthew appears nervous . . . shaking his leg around, tapping his foot, and just generally squirming around. After a few minutes, he lies down on the bench and sucks on his finger. He moves alone over by the door to the cafeteria and just sits there. . . . At 8:40, Ms. Hill calls level four students to line up and then the other levels in descending order. This is the way she calls them to line up for the remainder of the day. Matthew is first in line. The students walk in a single-file line and stop often. It appears that there are designated stop points because the students each seem to know exactly where to stop.

Once in class, there was a great deal of downtime, since both the teacher and the paraprofessional spent large amounts of time attending to paperwork and point sheets while these students, though designated as having EBD, were expected to sit quietly with no task in front of them and spend a total of approximately 2 hours each day waiting. Transitioning to electives (such as PE or art) or lunch was another time waster. Each time the students lined up to leave the room, it was at least 7 minutes before the line would actually start walking out of the room. Each time the students moved from one setting to another, they were expected to line up, re–line up, and stop in the line and wait for minutes at a time for no apparent reason. All the students, Matthew included, waited patiently and quietly in line each time they were told to do so. Transitions from one area to the next took approximately 20 minutes each, although one destination was no more than 2 minutes' walk from the other.

When actually in the classroom, there were portions of time (10–20 minutes at a time) when the teachers told the students to just sit quietly. One such example was during a math lesson:

From 2:05 to 2:10, Ms. Appleton has her group at the table in the front. She is grading papers and the students are sitting quietly. She keeps saying, "Guys, give me a minute." At 2:10 the boys start talking among themselves. Ms. Hill, the paraprofessional, yells from across the room, "Who's talking?" The room gets silent. Ms. Appleton turns to me and says, "See, the paras are your lifeline in EBD.". . . All the boys begin talking among themselves. They are telling each other jokes and each boy is off task, including Matthew. Ms. Hill is filling out point sheets and writing each student's homework down on the sheet. . . . Ms. Appleton leaves the room and the boys in her group are getting out of their seats and fooling around.

There were also similar chunks of time when Ms. Appleton left the room and Ms. Hill was left to monitor the students. During one such observation,

Ms. Hill told the students to take out a book and read. The problem here was that the students were not allowed to get out of their seats to select a new book. Matthew read a short book during this time and got out of his seat to try to select another book. He was reprimanded for doing so and told to go back to his seat. He then began to get restless in his seat.

Ms. Appleton admitted that Ms. Hill had better classroom control over the class. She had a strong, firm tone, and the students seemed to fear her. During one observation, the different management styles of the two were observed:

> Ms. Hill comes over. She grabs Owen by the arm and drags him out into the hallway to yell at him. Matthew jumps up out of his seat and starts going over to another student, but he sees me looking at him and stops and sits back down. Ms. Appleton comes back in and tells them that they will not be going to the Youth Fair if they misbehave. She has been making this threat all day. She has already told two of the students that they will not be going and continues to use it as a threat with those same students.

Although Ms. Hill actually spent more time than Ms. Appleton trying to instruct the students, her lack of training as a teacher was evident. During one observation of Matthew's reading group, the students were going to read the story "Cats Sleep Anywhere." Ms. Hill read each of the new vocabulary words listed in the book and had the students repeat each one after her. When she came to the word *stout*, she asked if any of the students knew what it meant, but none did. She suggested they look for it in the glossary, but it was not there. It became apparent that Ms. Hill did not know what the word meant when she told the students a stout was a type of nose that some animals have. One of the boys in the group said, "Isn't that a snout? This says *stout*." Ms. Hall then informed the students although it was spelled *stout*, it was pronounced *snout* and was a type of nose. This was the only vocabulary word that she defined for the students. After they read through the list together, each student read the list independently. Matthew read each of the words without a problem and aided other struggling students as they read.

Unfortunately, instruction by the teacher was no better than that offered by the paraprofessional. In reading, Ms. Appleton simply assigned pages for students to read by themselves and spent her time talking to other personnel or filing paperwork. In one observation, this was the case for the entire 90-minute reading period. In math, students were given an assigned list of problems and told that they would not be able to complete any work at home and that unfinished problems would be marked wrong. Then, the students were told to work independently, with no assistance, although they did not have the skills to complete the work.

Third-Grade Academics

In a math observation, Matthew was working on subtraction with regrouping. He worked each problem out in his head, concentrating on each and counting on his fingers without regrouping, writing down the wrong answer each time. Ms. Appleton looked at his paper and told him that he was not regrouping properly. She told him he needed to regroup, but she did not tell him how to do it. Instead, she continued grading other papers. Matthew clearly did not know how to regroup properly, since he continued to work hard on each problem again in the wrong way.

In September, Matthew scored 100% correct on a spelling test of 15 words, among them *red*, *get*, *penguin*, *elk*, and *said*. In March of that school year, he again earned 100%, this time with 15 much more difficult words, such as *river*, *froze*, *freeze*, *grabbed*, *waiting*, *tails*, and *bear*. His sentences included "The water in the lake is frozen" and "The coat is hanging on the hook." The work sample at the beginning of this chapter is an example of a paragraph he wrote in honor of Martin Luther King Jr. Day when he responded to a writing assignment to develop his own "dream." This example illustrates both his writing skills and his social concern. He seemed to see the helmets as a symbol of social status, as well as a protective item that all students should have.

When asked about the potential for mainstreaming, Ms. Appleton stated that she thought he was almost ready, but wanted to wait until he was in fourth grade because there was a particular teacher who she thought would be the right teacher for him. Matthew was reportedly performing on or close to grade level and had been functioning on the highest possible behavior level from the time he entered the class.

Fourth Grade

Matthew's fourth-grade year presented continuing concerns about the quality of his education in the special education program. Mrs. Appleton did not return to the school and her expectations of Matthew's possible mainstreaming were not being implemented. His new teacher, Ms. Gomez, reported that he had some minor behavior problems in the cafeteria (he received an indoor suspension for not following directions), and had one incident of "fighting" in the classroom. He received grades of B's and C's in his fourth-grade year, and at the middle of that year, he was functioning at the third-grade level in reading and high-third-grade level in math. Ms. Gomez informed us that his class was not participating in the state-mandated standardized test because it was "too high for these kids," but when Matthew took a practice version of the test, he was in the 48th percentile for math and 22nd percentile for reading at his grade level. While this may not match grade-level expectations, it did not meet the school district's requirements for alternative assessment.

When we asked Ms. Gomez about possibly mainstreaming Matthew, she stated that although his behavior was no problem, he was too low academically to try out the regular education classroom. She stated that he would be doing much better academically if there were more support at home, but that homework was not returned, point sheets were not returned, and his fourth grading period was plagued with absences. Ms. Gomez stated that Matthew turned in no homework because his mother was not home to monitor it. She added that she didn't grade homework, since most students did not turn it in. Matthew's mother told us that she wanted him to be mainstreamed as soon as possible. When we last saw Matthew he was still meeting all the behavioral goals in the EBD program and was performing close to grade level; however, there were no signs of mainstreaming ahead.

Questions

1. What role, if any, do you think that race and social class played in the placement process for Austin and Matthew?
2. Compare the referral and evaluation process for Matthew and Austin. Which aspects seem reasonable to you and which seem puzzling? What is your opinion of the placement outcomes for both boys?
3. If you were Ms. Jones, what (if anything) would you have done differently with Matthew and Austin?
4. What do you think attributed to the improvements in Matthew's behavior in the EBD program?
5. If you were Ms. Hanks, what strategies would you try to get Austin to perform in your class?
6. Research has shown that Black students in special education are more likely to be placed in more restrictive settings. Do you believe that it is beneficial for students to be in a more restricted setting if it allows for smaller numbers of students in a class? Consider the pros and cons of segregated settings for students with behavioral problems. Get in a group with two of your classmates and compare and discuss your notes.
7. Conduct a search for information on the history and current status of busing students for the purpose of racial desegregation. Are such mandates in place in your school district? What are some contrasting arguments regarding the impact of busing?

CHAPTER 7

Emotional/Behavior Disorder, Learning Disability, or English-Language Learner?

Edith: *"She's NOT handicap!"*

Born in the United States of Haitian parents, Edith had been exited from ESOL programming by the time we observed her in her third-grade class at Mabel Oakes Elementary School. Located in the southern end of the county, this school had a student mobility rate of 66%, and 99% of the students received free/reduced-price lunch. The student population comprised African American, Haitian, and Hispanic students, the last being mainly the children of migrant workers. Edith stood out in her class physically because she was very tall and overweight for her age, and was usually dressed in long skirts, which reflected the religious beliefs of her family. However, the data on her during that time are limited because, apart from her appearance, she did not stand out appreciably in terms of behavioral or academic difficulties. In the 2nd year of the study, the school counselor informed the researchers of Edith's EBD placement and expressed concern and surprise at this outcome.

FIRST YEAR OF THE STUDY: THIRD GRADE AT MABEL OAKS

A heavyset girl with large brown eyes and a broad, kind smile, Edith sat lethargically at the rear left of the classroom, adjacent to the wall. Most days, she actually faced the wall, with several objects in her vicinity to serve as a distraction to any instruction that may have been occurring at the front of

---

*Authors' note: This chapter was written by Juliet Hart.

the room. These mild diversions included the window above her desk, the class artwork next to her desk, the class plant terrariums on a table nearby, and the computers at the back of the room. When these objects were no longer interesting, Edith found ways to distract herself, including playing quietly with her water bottle, pencils, pens, pieces of paper, and hair.

EDITH GETS NOTICED: FOURTH GRADE AT MABEL OAKS

Although we did not observe Edith during her fourth-grade year, we gleaned much information about her referral and placement through interviews and informal conversations with her general education referring teacher, Mr. Peterson; her school counselor, Ms. Sanchez; and the school psychologist, Ms. Fernandez. Mr. Peterson reported, "I've known Edith since about first grade. You just couldn't miss her. I've got lots of Edith stories."

Mr. Peterson was a White male with a master's degree in ESOL education whose instructional and classroom management skills were rated by our research team as adequate. He had taught fourth grade for a number of years. He described Edith as "different":

> Well, you could just tell she was different. It was Halloween. Edith really made an impression that day. We had a teacher dress up as the cowardly lion from the *Wizard of Oz*, and Edith just freaked. I don't know what her situation was. The teacher's costume was very realistic. Edith was crying and making a complete ass of herself in the office all day.

Mr. Peterson did not comment on whether this might be a response conditioned by Edith's culture and religion. He did concede that "by fourth grade, she did dress up for Halloween, like a fairy princess. She got into the culture some more." While he mentioned Edith's involvement in occasional conflicts with her classmates, he indicated that "the kids picked on her and she had to defend herself." He also commented that "in my class, she only stuck out because of her size. Otherwise, she wasn't much different than anybody else. She was just lumped in with the dregs of society."

THE REFERRAL: TEACHER'S PERCEPTIONS

When asked about the reasons for Edith's referral for special education, Mr. Peterson stated:

She's got no attention span, no focus. I don't know that she was ever told "a school's purpose is this" or if she understood what education is for. Edith didn't seem to understand the reason for school. Kids come to school for a lot of different reasons—some come for meals or to get out of their parents' hair. If I could teach her social skills so she could get a job and not get fired, that's a goal. . . . Lots of kids at this school will become labor. We create blue collar here.

Expanding on his perceptions of the level of parental involvement and the family's understanding of schooling, he added:

There was no support for Edith. Her mom had two jobs, one of which was down in [a town about 30 miles away] as a maid. I suspect there were times when she did not even see her mom. She was practically raising herself and probably still is. I think she was more concerned with surviving. I did meet the mom at the staffing, but I threw the referral to the reading teacher because that's where her academic problems seemed serious. She initiated it; Edith was referred for her academic problems. I think when they did the testing, all of her other issues came up.

THE ASSESSMENT

Analysis of Edith's records and an interview with Ms. Fernandez, the psychologist, confirmed that Mr. Peterson had initially referred Edith "due to her poor academic performance and behavior difficulties at school." Intellectual functioning was determined to be in the low-average range, with deficits in reading and writing, and a relative strength in mathematics. Personality assessment was conducted using the usual projective battery, on the basis of which the psychologist concluded that Edith had EBD. Ms. Fernandez never mentioned conducting actual observations of Edith in her classroom or any other environment and there is no record of such observation in the report.

The psychologist's report indicated that Edith's response to a single item was of particular concern: To the statement "I feel like hurting myself," Edith responded, "All the time." As a result of her assessment, the psychologist concluded that Edith "presented as an unhappy youngster with a negative self-image" who "is experiencing a significant amount of emotional difficulties." During the interview, when asked about her impressions of Edith, Ms. Fernandez stated:

I can recall Edith somewhat. I remember because I had to do crisis intervention with her because she mentioned suicidal thoughts. She was a very needy child. She was somber, but at the same time, eager to please. She'd interact regardless of knowing me. She seeked attention and affection, was rejected by her peers. She didn't have a lot of positive interactions with her peers. I think she told me she wanted to kill herself, with a knife? [raised intonation]. I took the case seriously.

There was no record in the psychologist's report of Edith's stating she wanted to kill herself with a knife.

FAMILY PERSPECTIVES

The researchers paid several visits to the home and discovered a strong family unit, with Edith's mother, stepfather, and a total of six siblings living in a well-kept home about 5 miles away from the school to which Edith had been moved for the EBD program. Her original school was a short walk to her home. While the mother worked long hours, an elder sister was clearly in charge of daily housekeeping. Two of her siblings attended a local college, and two were in high school. Edith attended a Haitian church on a weekly basis and participated in Sunday school class and choir practice with a dozen other girls her age. One of the researchers went to church one Sunday with Edith and observed her in the Sunday school class, where she participated with full compliance, showing no distinction between her behaviors and those of her peers.

In a lengthy interview, Edith's mother emphatically disagreed with the school's assessment of Edith:

Edith is not handicap! . . . I tell them at school, Edith do lots for me at home. I send her to the store, she get everything I need, no problem. She listen at home and do what I tell her. She behave. She no have problem in the brain. She fine. I pray to God and she fine. I have six children. Two in college, two in high school, doing fine. I have a 4-year-old and he doing fine too. . . . There was these kids, bothering Edith every day, that's why. Edith come home, she cry every day. I go to the school, the principal don't do nothing about it. They tell me Edith have problem. So I take her to doctor. He say she fine. No handicap. I take her to another one. Same thing. I take her to three doctor. They all say she fine! They [school personnel] say Edith say she want to die, so she have problem. I tell them, kids been bothering

Edith every day and she cry, she upset. That why she say that. . . . She fine with me at home. She go to church every week. She walk with her cousins. She sing in the chorus at church. She going to be in a play at church in December 25. Edith, she OK. She fine. She need help with her reading and writing, but she not handicap. I went to the school [placement conference]. I am not agree with them about Edith. They tell me Edith cannot read and write, and she have problem. . . . They say she stay in program one year. She still there. If she need help to read, they should help her.

When we asked the psychologist if it was possible the mother was making a valid point about Edith's emotional difficulties, she acknowledged that they were "mostly school related." Ms. Fernandez said that Edith was upset because of her mother's insistence that she had to wear a skirt to school. Regarding Edith's threat to "kill herself," Ms. Fernandez felt that "if a child is making those kind of serious statements, there must be something more going on, and I don't think the mother recognized this." Regarding her perceptions of Edith's family involvement, Ms. Fernandez concluded, "Edith's parents need to continue becoming involved in her educational and emotional well-being."

SPECIAL EDUCATION DETERMINATION

Following the psychological assessment, placement for Edith in the EBD program was swift. In an interview regarding the mother's role in the staffing, Mr. Peterson reported, "The mother was there. She went along with everything. She may not have understood everything going on, although there was an interpreter there, a Haitian kindergarten teacher we have." When asked about her current school placement, Edith herself reported in an interview:

My mom want me to go to Sunny Acres Middle by my house, 'cause I could walk, but I got to go to Lafayette [school with EBD program to which she was bused]. One day I came home from school. My mom said I have to go to Lafayette because they gave her a paper that I'm supposed to go.

Ms. Sanchez, the school counselor from Edith's referring school, stated:

We have a majority of students who are minorities and who are from the migrant community. . . . One of the biggest problems is that the people from these communities will sign away anything, and they don't know the questions to ask. Some of the parents come in and they're so confused, and they ask me, "What's this paper? What do I do?" I imagine Edith's mom just signed whatever paperwork she was given.

Relaying further her feelings about the appropriateness of Edith's EBD placement, Ms. Sanchez stated:

In my heart, I believe it was wrong, inappropriate. When Edith was here, she knew who she could come to. The counseling services she was referred for [counseling program] were not forthcoming. That wasn't her fault. This is a full-service school. She could get services she needed right here. Now she travels out of her community to another school, where she doesn't have those connections. I think the worst part is that there was absolutely no closure for her. One day she was here, and the next day she was just gone. The child will experience that as 'There must be something wrong with me. They sent me away.' She had a caring nest here at Mabel Oakes. She doesn't have that anymore.

THE PLACEMENT: BEHAVIOR MANAGEMENT IN A RESTRICTIVE ENVIRONMENT

Edith began her self-contained fifth-grade EBD placement the following fall at Lafayette Elementary School, a school similar demographically to her home school. Lafayette is a relatively large building that has a center courtyard with well-kept grass and trees. Edith's EBD class was located out in the portables at some distance from the main building and common areas such as the office, cafeteria, and library.

The EBD teacher was Mr. Donovan, a handsome, heavyset Black man with a booming voice, shaved head, and wide smile. He commented on having several years of teaching experience, though it was unclear whether he was certified to teach students with EBD. He was the behavior management teacher for the EBD unit at the school, and he remarked that he likely would seek an administrative position in the near future. He described the students in the program:

Well, we get a lot of students just out of control. We want to give them self-worth, and reinforce them to feel good about themselves. You've got to control them. You've got to allow them to learn according to their modalities. A big issue here is new staff. They're not trained with safe physical management. . . . They're apprehensive. There's steps to it. You've got to calm them down, use nonverbal, verbal, touch, gestures, speaking calm. You, the teacher, need to back into the corner, not back the kid in the corner. You have to avoid confrontation.

Our observations of this classroom revealed daily instructional and organizational routines based totally on teacher control. Routines included supervised breakfast in the cafeteria at a later time than that of the general education population and supervised bathroom breaks at specified times. Students were required to line up daily to have their pencils sharpened by the teacher or aide; to line up by behavioral level for out-of-class activities; and when transitioning, to keep a specified distance between themselves and the next student.

Our observations of Mr. Donovan's management style contrasted sharply with his own description, as in the following excerpt:

As I approached Mr. Donovan's class as they walked from the cafeteria, he yelled, "File the line!" Students are required to keep a distance of [approximately] 3 feet and to be silent, hands at their sides. One student was sent to the back of the line for failing to keep the distance rule. Edith reported that a student called her a name. This student was also sent to the back of the line. Mr. Donovan yelled to the student, "You are off level!" And to the paraprofessional he instructed, "Add him another day! You keep it up, and you and me will be on the floor today! If this line is not in order, I'll cancel PE!"

In addition to *file the line*, Mr. Donovan and his assistant frequently used commands and threats such as *Heads down, Bury your face, You're off level, You just got three extra days, PE is canceled, Stand in the corner, Give him zeroes, I'll give you something to cry about,* and *You and me will be on the floor.* Staff would also use physical intimidation tactics, such as the teacher and assistant walking menacingly toward students, grabbing student's faces, the teacher's banging of a chair or desk en route to deal with an off-task student, and the use of physical restraint with students for "becoming verbally disrespectful" (as reported by Mr. Donovan).

SCHEDULE

The restrictive nature of the EBD program was manifested in several ways. Since separate scheduling resulted in the students returning from breakfast no earlier than 9:05 A.M., and as late as 9:15 A.M., they received 35–45 fewer instructional minutes than did their nondisabled peers. They attended only one class, PE, with the general education students, and whenever Mr. Donovan did not "cancel PE," he would accompany the students to "show his face," in order to "keep his students in line." Instruction in music and art was delivered to these students in the self-contained setting.

When asked about possible mainstreaming for students, Mr. Donovan replied, "I'm a big advocate for inclusion. We don't want our kids isolated. We've had some students be very successful." However, out of 14 students in Edith's class, none was mainstreamed in any subject area. With regard to Edith, Mr. Donovan reported that she was "doing great" and "has really improved." However, when asked about her possible return to the mainstream, Mr. Donovan said, "Maybe she'll be *partially* mainstreamed by high school."

EDITH'S EDUCATIONAL NEEDS:
THE INSTRUCTIONAL ENVIRONMENT

Although Mr. Donovan occasionally provided instruction that resonated with his students, the majority of his instruction was of the worksheet variety. When whole-group instruction did occur, Edith was often silent, though attentive, appearing not to understand or to be able to keep up with the rest of the group. Our field notes illustrated that during reading activities, Edith was commonly "staring off," "silent," "flipping pages," or "grimacing." Her off-task behavior seemed to be related to lack of understanding of content or difficulty with written language rather than purposeful misbehavior.

Although Edith's work samples were extremely difficult to decipher, she received average grades and little corrective feedback. For example, she received "happy faces" on journal essays that were barely comprehensible. The class was using a fifth-grade basal text, but both Mr. Donovan's reports and our testing on the Woodcock Johnson Test in reading established Edith's level at close to third grade (3.1 for letter-word identification and 2.8 for passage comprehension). When she failed an accelerated reading test based on a book that was beyond her level, Mr. Donovan reported, "I pass her with D's because she tries." When asked about addressing Edith's academic needs, Mr. Donovan reported, "I taught the kids context clues to help them," explaining that he did this so that his students would be more successful in taking the state standardized assessment. Edith's performance on that test was in the third percentile for reading and in the fifth percentile for mathematics problem solving.

Mr. Donovan, like the referring teacher, Mr. Peterson, reported that Edith "speaks the language well," and has "made much improvement." However, her work samples, class participation, grades, and conversations evidenced both written and oral language proficiency problems. For example, in Edith's interview, her language suggested an interplay of influences from her first language and African American Vernacular English such as "We play bowling," "We set up the carpet," "We put ten bowlers there," "When is nighttime I be scared," "But I only fight one time," "On Christmas I get gifts and go to places," and "She don't tell me why." These difficulties with tense, subject-verb agreement, and vocabulary were not addressed in her educational program.

EDITH'S RESPONSES TO BEHAVIOR MANAGEMENT

The focus of the EBD program was on behavior, and our observations showed Edith as consistently and quietly compliant with staff directions or reprimands. The fact that she was usually quietly off task during instruction presented a contrast to many of the other students in the EBD program, who tended to react sarcastically to staff reprimands or who were repeatedly disciplined for verbal disrespect, disobedience, and aggression. Across 16 classroom observations of Edith during her fifth-grade year, the only indication of troubling behavior was a report from school personnel that Edith had had to be "taken down" (physically restrained) for "foul language" and "telling lies on the other kids." Mr. Donovan added:

> Immediately, she went home and told her family about it. Her brother came out to the school to ask why. Her mom didn't know Edith could be restrained. . . . At the staffing, parents are told what *could* happen. They don't raise questions. It's possible she didn't understand the language, although we have a Haitian Creole person to translate.

Edith described the restraint, stating:

> I been restrained one time. A girl, Ayesha, want to fight me. Her and her auntie want to double-team me. They told the teacher. I was already cool down and they restrain me and my momma got mad, because I didn't do nothin' to the girl. Plus, I got surgery on my leg and my hand was hurting. I got pins on my legs. My mom told my brother to come and tell them don't restrain anymore. I don't like the school at all.

During an interview with one of the researchers, it turned out that Mr. Donovan was unaware of Edith's history of surgery, although this information was in her cumulative file.

Mr. Donovan's views of Edith's family were similar to those of Ms. Fernandez, the school psychologist. He stated that Edith's parent was one of those "who don't show up." However, Mr. Donovan also related that the mother sent the child's adult brother to school on the only occasion that there was a disciplinary issue to be addressed and consistently signed the daily home note and point sheet. When asked if he had attempted to schedule a parent conference, Mr. Donovan stated, "I think I tried to schedule a conference for her IEP. I'm sure I did. Let's check the cum." Upon checking the cumulative file, Mr. Donovan found no record that he had scheduled a conference.

Edith continued in the EBD program on into middle school, at a school at some distance from her home. Readers are encouraged to refer to Hart (2003) for follow-up on her case and a description of the quality of her special education middle school placement.

Questions

1. Review the definition for EBD. Do you feel that Edith is a student with EBD? Why or why not?
2. In recent years, there have been many cases that have made national headlines of students who were ridiculed and who reacted by "striking back" with acting-out behavior. Do an online search of local newspapers to find at least one such case in the past 5 years. What do you think might account for such behavior? Report the case you find back to your class.
3. If you were hired as an advocate for Edith's family, what recommendations would you have made to Edith's mother? What types of services might you have suggested to assist Edith?
4. Edith's placement at Lafayette employed a behavioral system for students with EBD. What was your opinion of the behavioral system in place? Do you think this system worked for Edith? Why or why not?
5. Pretend you were hired to be Edith's general education teacher. How would you address the cultural discontinuities evident in many of the school personnel's perceptions of Edith's family? How would you address the issue of peer teasing?

CHAPTER 8

Attention Deficit Hyperactivity Disorder, Emotional/Behavior Disorder, or Learning Disability?

Paul: *"I don't want this case to go EBD."*

> He can do the work, but I have to sit with him for it to get done, or he
> won't do it. He has trouble staying in his seat. He has a short attention
> span. But he is able to learn. (Paul's first-grade teacher at his staffing)

Paul was an adorably impish 5-year-old Hispanic kindergartner with a kind disposition. Quite squirmy and frequently out of his seat, he seemed to have trouble concentrating. As a native Spanish speaker classified as ESOL Level 4, Paul had very good but not fully proficient English-language skills, according to the district's criteria.

Paul attended a dual-immersion program at Bay Vista Elementary, where he received instruction in Spanish for half his school day, from one teacher, and in English for the other half, from a different teacher. Both his teachers were excellent. Ms. Chaney, who taught the English half, was from Jamaica. Ms. Flores, who taught the Spanish half, was Hispanic, and a native Spanish speaker.

Bay Vista was widely considered to be an effective school. This was based on a long-standing reputation as well as the school's performance on the state's new accountability measures. We consistently noted high-quality instruction and management across classrooms. The school's student population at the time of our study was almost all Hispanic and of varying socioeconomic levels.

Paul's kindergarten teachers referred him to the school's child study team (CST) early in the year, primarily for concerns about his emotional and behavioral functioning. The first CST meeting was held in November, and the second in mid-March. The following year, Paul was promoted to the first grade and was evaluated for a possible special education placement early in the fall. In mid-November, he was placed in the school's special education program for children with LD. Soon thereafter he began attending the school's resource room for part of each day.

A consistent picture of Paul emerged during our many observations over a 2-year period. Academically, he appeared to be stronger in reading and language arts than in math. He was successful at many assignments, but needed assistance with others. He seemed to have difficulty focusing on the task at hand. His teachers described him as capable and intelligent, but inconsistent in his work. He was sociable with his peers, almost always interacting in a positive manner. In a situation in which he easily could have become angered, he instead demonstrated kindness. A neighbor grabbed Paul's pencil out of his hand while he was using it, so that he could use the eraser. Paul then handed the boy a different eraser, saying, "Here, take this one. It's better."

Paul's parents were divorced. He lived with his mother, Sylvia, and one older brother. A second older brother lived with an aunt. Sylvia shared with us that she was ill, suffering from depression and nervous breakdowns. When Paul was in first grade she brought a letter from her doctor to the school explaining that she was not able to help Paul with his homework, and not to pressure her. Paul's father, José, occasionally helped care for him, particularly when his mother was not feeling well. José agreed to attend school meetings because Sylvia found them to be quite unsettling. She told us that she was unhappy with Paul's school; for second grade she moved him to a private school. After this, we were unable to contact the family for permission to continue the study.

PAUL'S KINDERGARTEN YEAR:
CONCERNS ABOUT BEHAVIOR

When we first visited all the primary classrooms in our schools in September, we asked teachers if there were any students about whom they were already concerned and thinking of referring to the CST. When we asked Ms. Flores this question, she said that she had one "concern," and discreetly pointed out Paul. We asked teachers to tell us if their concerns were primarily about academics, behavior, or both. In Paul's case, both his teachers unequivocally said, "behavior." In February, Ms. Chaney, Paul's other kindergarten teacher, conveyed:

> In the beginning, his behavior was destructive. He cut things he wasn't supposed to, ate glue, and was self-destructive. He used to not be able to sit in his seat. Since I met with the mom, he has been doing much better. He still needs constant directing, every day, with

everything, but he's getting better. Whenever he gets a thought in his head, he blurts it out.

She reported they had turned the paperwork in, met with the assistant principal, and held the first CST. They had checked to see if, since Paul was bilingual, his Spanish was a "problem." They had already met with the school's counselors several times and with someone from the Department of Health and Rehabilitative Services. She added, "The mother isn't too fond of us because we needed to call her in."

We observed Paul many times during his kindergarten year. During each observation we noted a different aspect of his personality and behavior. He was active and, at times, anxious to please. On one occasion we watched him and the rest of his class in the library while the librarian was reading a story. We noted:

> Paul is now standing up, behind the librarian's right shoulder, while she reads. He's looking at books on the shelf, and now walks behind her chair. She finally turns to him and says something quietly. He continues standing there. She turns back to the other students, who now are more restless, but still paying attention.

Another time we accompanied Paul and his class to the cafeteria and sat at the same table as Paul. As they finished eating, many students took books from the baskets that had been placed in the middle of the tables. Paul did not. Ms. Flores then came over and sat by us. She told us about a student who was on medication for hyperactivity, "but shouldn't be." She added, "I wish I could switch the medication from her to Paul—he's the one who really needs it." . . . Paul threw an apple in the general direction of the trash can. It missed. The intern said sternly, "Paul," and he went over and picked it up and threw it in the trash. We walked back to the classroom and the students returned to their seats. They were expected to select a book from the baskets on their tables and read silently. Paul got up and went to get a book from another table. The intern told him to return to his seat. He fell on the floor, apparently on purpose, and then went over to his seat but did not sit. He knelt, stood, and then rocked back and forth.

During another observation, the class was playing a quick game in the few minutes before the bell rang for dismissal. The teacher had written various numbers on the board, scattered and in random order. She would say, "Papa caliente" (Hot potato), and "El numero 1" (Number 1 [or another number]) while throwing a beanbag to a student, who was supposed to catch it and then go up to the board and cross out the number she had said. Whenever a student was successful the rest of the class cheered. When it was Paul's turn, he correctly crossed out the 5. Then it was time for everyone to line up. Paul did, but then left the line to pick up some little scraps of paper the room's big fans had blown onto the floor and put them back into the trash. The teacher saw him and said, "Thank you, Paul, thank you!"

During one of our last observations of the year, the teacher told the class that they were about to do something special and that she had a magic word. She said, with much enthusiasm, "Científicos!" (scientists). She asked what it meant. A student said, "Locos" (crazy). The teacher said no. Paul asked, "Mágicos?" (magicians). "No." After other incorrect responses, the teacher told them, "Son personas importantes que hacen experimentos" (They are important people who do experiments). She said this last word in a louder voice, after a slight pause, building suspense. "Like discovering medicine. They are the ones who observed that plants need water and sun to grow." As the lesson continued, Paul seemed to be trying to pay attention, but was having trouble sitting still—he began kneeling on his chair. The teacher told them they were going to be scientists and put on their thinking caps, special glasses, special gloves, and lab coats. She demonstrated all this in pantomime. In contrast to his peers, who were fully engaged, Paul continued to become more fidgety, until he was almost lying on his table. The teacher praised someone else for sitting still and Paul immediately sat up straight. Then he began playing with the clothespins given to him as rewards for good behavior, to be exchanged later for a prize. The teacher directed him to return one to the basket.

PAUL'S SECOND CST MEETING

Having missed the first CST meeting for Paul, we were glad we could observe the second one, held in March in his kindergarten year. The assistant principal, a counselor, the psychologist, and both kindergarten teachers were present. The mother was not there when the meeting was supposed to begin; she called on the phone soon thereafter to say that she would not be able to attend. The psychologist urged her to attend, telling her that her signature would be needed. She said she would come in after all.

While waiting for the meeting to begin, the psychologist showed the researcher the referral form. The teachers' primary concerns for Paul were an "inability to follow directions, distractible behavior, and a short attention span." She had cross-referenced the reports, looking at what teachers had written as their primary concerns and then checking the behavior rating scale to see if these results were consistent with what the teachers had said. They were.

The psychologist asked the teachers for more information about Paul. They explained that he "needed constant supervision" and was "impulsive."

He had days when he did do well, but only with the teacher there to redirect him. "He is able to do the work when someone is on top of him constantly."

When Paul's mother, Sylvia, arrived, the meeting proceeded in Spanish, even though Ms. Chaney was not bilingual. The psychologist told Sylvia that Paul was very "inquieto" (fidgety). She asked how he was at home, and Sylvia said, "Lo mismo" (the same), and explained that she had talked to the doctor about how Paul had trouble concentrating. The psychologist responded that it was time to bring in more professionals, that at the school they could help with the educational aspects of Paul's needs, but that a medical doctor was needed to help with other aspects. "Otherwise, school will just get harder and harder for Paul. Paul's hyperactivity is something that requires a doctor." She was clearly pushing for Paul to be put on medication for hyperactivity.

Sylvia reported that Paul had been tested for a language disability, but that they had not given her a copy of the report. Later she said that he was also tested by a psychiatrist. The classroom teacher shared a copy of a work sample that he completed while in a preschool program, and the psychologist recognized it as something that would have been completed with a speech and language therapist.

The psychologist recommended proceeding with a formal evaluation. The counselor had Paul's mother sign forms giving permission to obtain the Head Start report and to conduct an evaluation. Very little explanation was provided about what the forms entailed. Sylvia left after she had signed the forms, as if there had been an agreement that she was there to sign forms and then would be free to leave. When she had left, almost the first thing the psychologist said was, "She's been aware of it and she's been avoiding it."

PAUL'S FIRST-GRADE YEAR

Although we observed Paul numerous times in his first-grade general education classrooms as well as in his special education class after he was placed, space does not permit our describing these observations here. His behaviors were similar to those we observed the previous year—he was distractible and playful and needed assistance to stay on task and do his work. Some days he seemed more agitated than others, and he especially became more anxious toward the end of his first-grade year. He particularly bonded with his first-grade Spanish-speaking teacher, who looked out for him and described him as "sweet." She thought that after he started attending special education classes his behavior was "a little off." When asked how he was adjusting, she said, "He's having a hard time with it. It's so many changes for him."

PAUL'S PLACEMENT CONFERENCE

Paul's placement conference was held in mid-November. Notably, we were the only ones in attendance who had also been at the CST meeting, with the exception of the assistant principal. In addition, a placement specialist from the district office was there, as well as a different psychologist, a different counselor, a counselor intern, Paul's two first-grade teachers, the special education teacher, and Paul's father. The father attended the meeting instead of the mother because she was sick. He only spoke Spanish, and so the staffing specialist offered to translate because not everyone was bilingual.

When asked how Paul behaved at home, the father said that he was very active and played Nintendo a lot. He did not always want to finish his homework, but usually did. Next the assistant principal asked about his class work, and one teacher noted that he was "very distractible" and had trouble finishing his work. The second teacher added that she had him sitting in front.

> He can do the work, but I have to sit with him for it to get done, or he won't do it. He has trouble staying in his seat. He has a short attention span. But he is able to learn. He is more than capable to do his work. I don't know what it is, if he's immature or lazy, but he's capable.

Then the psychologist shared her report. She noted that Paul was quiet during the testing session and it was easy to establish rapport with him. But he was easily distracted, had trouble staying on task, and would play with his pencil or anything else he could find. She said that she repeated instructions in English and Spanish, but that Paul's comprehension was poor. She asked if he was receiving speech therapy. He was not. When she asked if he had ever been in speech therapy, no one seemed to know. Therefore, when others at the table responded that they did not think so, the researcher interjected, saying that he had, in preschool, since there had been a long discussion about this at the second CST meeting and it was relevant information. Given that Paul had previously received speech and language services, it was surprising that a speech therapist did not assess Paul as part of this evaluation. The psychologist added that his sentence construction was poor. She did not raise the likely possibility that Paul's oral language skills were affected by his limited English proficiency.

The psychologist then shared test results:

- WISC III (English): Verbal score = 83; performance score = 90; composite = 85. Strengths in vocabulary (11), block design (11), and object assembly (10). Weaknesses in comprehension (4) and picture arrangement (6).

- Wechsler Individual Achievement Test (WIAT): reading composite score = 98; basic reading = 94; reading comprehension = 87; spelling = 101; math composite = 85; math reasoning = 84; numerical operations = 97.
- Bender: 85.
- Kinetic Family Drawing Test: Paul did not include himself (an indication of low self-concept, according to the psychologist). The psychologist explained that Paul considered his mother to be the most important person in his life, and then his grandfather, and then his brother.

The psychologist concluded that Paul's intelligence was in the low-normal range and that he had a comprehension deficit. The written report indicated that Paul was at ESOL Level 4 and that his primary language was Spanish. Paul did not learn to speak until the age of 3. However, language-acquisition issues were not mentioned elsewhere in the report. Nor were they discussed at the placement conference.

The staffing specialist then explained that Paul qualified for LD because he needed individual attention and had "learning process deficits." She said that he had been referred for "poor academic performance." This statement contradicted the information on the kindergarten teachers' referral forms and was inconsistent with their statements about their concerns, as well as with other information presented at his CST meeting. The school district's criteria for LD placement stipulated that students must show a discrepancy between their potential, as measured by an intelligence test, and their academic achievement. Notably, Paul's achievement test scores were actually higher than his intelligence test scores. The assistant principal leaned over and pointed this out to the researcher, whispering, "Isn't the discrepancy supposed to go the other way?"

The psychologist advised José that Paul should see a doctor for medicine for his hyperactivity. While she was explaining this, Paul came in and climbed on his father's lap. The psychologist continued, saying that Paul should see a psychiatrist to determine why he was depressed and distracted. She explained that these were symptoms. The counselor then sent Paul into the room next door to wait. The psychologist continued, explaining the symptoms of depression, and stating that Paul was exhibiting these. José seemed to become upset, saying that he thought this meeting was supposed to be about helping Paul with his schoolwork. He explained that Paul's mother suffered from depression. The psychologist nodded, saying, "It can run in families." Again she spoke about the symptoms of masked depression: distractible, fidgety, having trouble sleeping, having eating problems. She said that a psychiatrist could determine if Paul's difficulties concentrating and lack of progress were caused by emotional problems. Yet there was no indication that a psychiatrist's opinion had been sought as part of the placement decision.

Then the staffing specialist explained the special education program and asked the father if he understood. The father said, "Sí," and signed the form put in front of him giving permission for Paul to be in an LD program. Then he left.

After the father had gone, the psychologist said that she thought Paul was clinically depressed, but that she did not write this in her report because she did not want his case "to go EBD." In other words, she did not want him placed in a program for children with EBD. She later explained that she preferred the LD category "because she liked to rule that out first as the explanation for depression, rather than going right away with the more restrictive placement."

Questions

1. Review the current definitions of LD, EBD, and ADHD in the *Diagnostic and Statistical Manual of Mental Disorders*, fourth edition (*DSM-IV*). Do you think Paul's multidisciplinary team had enough information to determine whether he had one of these disabilities? With a partner, make a list of the information available to the team. What additional information might have been helpful? If you had been on the multidisciplinary team, what would you have recommended?

2. What do you think accounts for the change of tone between Paul's CST and the placement conference? List all the inconsistencies and discuss your list with a partner. How might these changes have affected Paul's placement?

3. How do you think Paul's case was influenced by his being an English-language learner? Think of as many ways as you can, and discuss these with a partner. Personnel at Paul's school believed that it is easier to determine if a child has a disability when he or she is in a bilingual program. Why do you think they said this? What are the implications of this for Paul?

4. Based on the information presented to you in this case, do you feel that the psychologist made the right decision to keep Paul from "going EBD?" Discuss the advantages/disadvantages to a placement that focuses on emotional needs versus a program that focuses on learning needs.

5. How closely should multidisciplinary teams follow established procedures and identification criteria when determining who qualifies for special education? Should it be acceptable to put a student in a program for which he or she has not really qualified in order to get the child help? Should we need to label students in order to get them extra assistance? How else could support services be delivered?

CHAPTER 9

Educable Mentally Retarded, English-Language Learner, or Ignored?

Clementina: *"I don't want to do no work!"*

The kindergarten teacher referred her! . . . Clementina was referred a long time ago! But the staffing just took place today!? (From Clementina's staffing, May, 4th grade)

When we first met her, Clementina was a demure third grader at an inner-city, predominantly Black school with a growing Hispanic population. She was born in the southeastern United States to Puerto Rican parents and spoke Spanish at home. Although it was not clear what her ESOL level was considered to be, she was in her school's third-grade class for English-language learners, with a Spanish-speaking teacher of Cuban heritage. By the time of her placement conference in the fourth grade, she had been exited from ESOL.

Clementina's school, Beecher Stowe Elementary, was located in a neighborhood considered by many to be "unsafe," with many rundown apartment buildings and industrial warehouses. The grounds were bare, not planted with shrubs and flowers like those of many other schools. Virtually the entire student body received free lunches. School personnel reported that many students came from single-parent homes or lived with someone other than a parent (such as a grandparent), had lost a parent to violence (for example, a shooting), had a close relative who was currently or had recently been incarcerated, had relatives who used street drugs, or had a combination of these factors. School personnel believed they had seen changes in the student body over the years; students had become "angrier" and discipline had become increasingly difficult. Many of the staff members had attended Stowe themselves.

Clementina lived with her mother, named Rosa, and with seven siblings and a nephew (her older sister's infant son). Her father was reportedly in Puerto Rico. We were told that an older brother and an older sister had been in jail for drug dealing. Her aunt lived close by and attended meetings at the school with Rosa and helped the family in many ways. Rosa herself had never attended school and was illiterate. She did not work, but lived on governmental assistance and stayed home to care for her children. Clementina's teacher told us, "The mother is retarded, and can't even sign her name, and she has eight kids. Clementina's older sister is 14, and now having a baby."

Clementina was absent for weeks at a time because of head lice. Her third-grade teacher told us, "Clementina was out all last week with head lice, and came back today, and was sent home again because she still has them." On another occasion she was not there because she had ringworm and was absent for several days. When asked at her staffing why Clementina was absent from school so often, Clementina's mother, Rosa, replied, "I don't know, she doesn't want to wake up and does not pay attention to me." When it was suggested that perhaps Clementina was sick, Rosa answered, "No, she does not complain of anything."

CLASSROOM OBSERVATIONS AND CONVERSATIONS WITH TEACHERS

Our observations of Clementina in her general education classes suggested that she only occasionally participated in class activities. We noted that the classroom instruction was adequate, though not particularly inspiring. Our overall impression of Clementina was of general disengagement. Each of the following examples is from a different observation during her third-grade year:

- Clementina was sitting at her desk with a passive, blank look on her face while classmates around her wrote in their journals. Her desk was empty. Ms. Gutierrez, her teacher, asked, "What are you writing about?" Clementina responded, "I don't have no journal." The teacher responded, "This is not an art class. You'd better write."
- We went over and checked Clementina's work. She smiled mischievously and confided, "I'm not doing my work." When asked, "Why not?" she answered, "I don't feel like it." She continued to just sit, looking at another student. A few minutes later, she was still sitting at her seat, doing nothing. The teacher ignored her.
- Another student, Floyd, shouted across the room, "Clementina, you got one?" (referring to a times table sheet students were supposed to be using to find the answers to basic multiplication problems). Clementina responded, "I don't want to do no work." Floyd laughed. The teacher scolded, "Floyd, don't laugh. She can do it the same way you are doing it."

- I went over and checked Clementina's paper and saw that she had written the first sentence. I told her, "Good." She pointed to what she had copied from the book and smiled up at me.

Ms. Gutierrez was concerned that Clementina was becoming increasingly restless and even aggressive as the year progressed. She told us that "she has really changed, become very aggressive, and is not the sweet little girl she used to be." By the end of the year she had moved Clementina's desk so that she was sitting apart from her classmates.

We continued observing Clementina the following year, in her fourth-grade general education class. She again was in a class with a bilingual Hispanic teacher, Ms. Carrillo. As in the previous year, the instruction seemed adequate, but not exceptional. We observed much the same pattern of minimal engagement:

- As the teacher pointed to each part of the diagram, the students spoke in unison. Clementina spoke as well, and appeared to be parroting what the others around her were saying.
- As Ms. Carrillo continued to go over the various points of finding the main idea and supporting details/ideas of a paragraph, Clementina looked at her workbook and then placed her head on her workbook. The teacher directed students to read the following story in the book silently. Approximately 3 minutes passed and Clementina still had her head down. "All right, what is the main idea?" the teacher asked. Several students raised their hands. Clementina did not. She lifted her head and began digging around in her book bag and fidgeting at her desk.

Ms. Carrillo was quite frustrated that Clementina had not been retained. In exasperation, she told us:

Last year Clementina got all F's in reading but then she received a C [on her report card]. A D is passing. So she got promoted. I don't know how, for Clementina reads on a first-grade reading level. She is low. . . . The whole process I find very frustrating.

When we asked in December if Clementina would be promoted to the fifth grade, she responded:

I can't say. Let's leave it at that. There is a lot of documentation that is required before a child can be retained. You ask me, she should be retained. She is very low. And when she takes the [state tests] she is going to be low. There's the issue of accountability and I have a lot of low kids. But when the scores come out, it will be considered my fault that they are so low. Everything is my fault.

FIRST CHILD STUDY TEAM MEETING

Ms. Carrillo's frustration was not surprising when we consider the slowness of the referral process in Clementina's case. Her first CST was held in April of the third grade, yet a year later there had been no progress on her referral.

Clementina's first CST meeting lasted only about 5 minutes. We entered the room at the time the meeting was to start, with the classroom teacher, and noted that someone was interviewing Clementina's mother, in Spanish. The questions all seemed related to language use, and whether Clementina and her sister used Spanish with the mother, friends, and one another. The mother, Rosa, was saying that Clementina and her sister spoke Spanish with her, but English with one another and their friends. They both started learning English when they were 5 and started school. Rosa was not aware that the girls were getting some instruction in Spanish (answering no to this question when in fact the girls did attend pull-out Spanish classes for Spanish speakers).

While this interview was taking place, the assistant principal asked the classroom teacher to sit close to her, and she went over the referral form with her, showing her where she should have written dates and put more information on the form. And then Rosa got up and left, and that was it. There was no group dialogue. No one explained the referral form to Rosa or told her what her rights as a parent were. No one asked her how Clementina was doing at home; no one explained to her how Clementina was doing in school. There was no discussion of prereferral intervention strategies. We asked the classroom teacher afterward if she thought maybe we had missed part of the meeting. She replied that she did not think so; she thought that they rushed through the meeting because they figured the parent would not understand anyway.

PLACEMENT CONFERENCE*

Clementina was evaluated more than a year after her third-grade teacher had referred her. Her staffing took place in May and was attended by a staffing specialist from the district office; the psychologist; the school counselor; the

---

*The school district used the term *staffing* for the special education placement conference. Other possible names for this meeting include *multidisciplinary team meeting* and *IEP meeting*.

assistant principal; Clementina's fourth-grade teacher; the special education teacher (for the school's self-contained EMH class); Clementina's mother, Rosa; her aunt, Maria; and two researchers.

While we waited in the office for the meeting to start, the assistant principal greeted us and said, "Let's see if she's going to show up today." Rosa and Maria arrived right on time at 9 A.M. "You're here," remarked the assistant principal, adding, "We are not ready to start. The psychologist isn't here." The meeting began at about 9:20, when the psychologist arrived.

As everyone was settling into their chairs around a small table, the staffing specialist asked, "Does Mom need a translator?" The classroom teacher responded, "Yes, I'll do it." While thumbing through Clementina's paperwork, the staffing specialist asked, "Has he always been in this school?" Rosa answered, "Yes, Clementina has been at this school since kindergarten." The staffing specialist continued, "How did he do in kindergarten? What were his grades?" The classroom teacher asked to see Clementina's records. As she looked through the papers, she exclaimed with surprise, "The kindergarten teacher referred her! Clementina was referred at kindergarten!" The staffing specialist responded, "Oh, I'm sorry. I said *he* instead of *she*. She's not a boy. Is this the first time she's been staffed?" She then looked at the assistant principal. The teacher responded, "Yes." The staffing specialist said, incredulously, "Clementina was referred a long time ago! But the staffing just took place today!?" Once again she looked to the assistant principal for a response. The assistant principal replied, "It's because of the bilingual assessment. You know how long those can take. We were waiting for that to be done." The staffing specialist responded, "So the bilingual assessment is what held up the process."

The psychologist shared results from the WISC-Revised:

> Nothing remarkable, no mental delays, she smiles when you look at her but she does not speak. She forgets things very easily. The average IQ is between 90 and 109. Clementina's full-scale IQ score is 51. She is in the mentally deficient range. Clementina has limited formal educational skills. She has some letter-word identification— she recognized letters but not words. She is at the kindergarten level.

The classroom teacher confirmed that Clementina was very low. She was able to write her first and last name, but sometimes inverted letters, such as the last letter of her surname. She knew the numbers from 1 to 20 and recognized colors. The staffing specialist asked, "Are there any words that she recognizes in class?" The classroom teacher responded, "I'm sure she recognizes the words *math* and *add*." The psychologist said:

> She did 1-digit addition but no subtraction in the math computation segment. She scored 48, kindergarten level. . . . On applied problems,

she was unable to tell time by the hour or count money. She could write letters but not words. On the Bender Visual Motor, her fine-motor-skills score was 52. She may have fine-motor problems. Her vision was tested. It was 20/30 in both eyes. So both her eyes appear to be OK, but not perfect. . . . She has an immature personality.

The staffing specialist concluded, with emphasis, "She is EMR." Although the district's guidelines stipulated that an evaluation for possible placement in an EMR program should include an adaptive-behavior scale, this had not been done. Thus, the multidisciplinary team did not have a complete picture of Clementina's functioning outside school and applied the label of EMR on the basis of test scores and school performance alone. Also, that Clementina was frequently absent and missed weeks of school at a time was not discussed as a possible reason for her being so low. Nor was it discussed that Clementina spoke Spanish as her first language and continued to speak Spanish at home with her mother. Although the assistant principal said that the reason it had taken so long to evaluate her was that the school had been waiting for the bilingual assessment, in fact the results of this assessment were not mentioned at the meeting. We could not find a bilingual assessor's report in her file. Clementina was evaluated in English only, despite the district's policy that students who have recently exited from ESOL should be evaluated bilingually.

The staffing specialist went on to say that Clementina needed to be in a smaller class and would be placed in the school's self-contained EMR class. Rosa was not asked for her opinion about this; rather, it appeared that the decision had been made ahead of time and the purpose of the meeting was to convey information and obtain her written permission for special education placement rather than involve her in the decision-making process. The staffing specialist added that Clementina would receive special door-to-door bus transportation. Rosa and Maria were pleased with this benefit.

While the psychologist was reading Clementina's test results, the special education teacher had been writing the goals and objectives for the IEP. When she finished, she made copies of the IEP and psychological report for Rosa. She asked, "Can they get this in Spanish?" The staffing specialist replied, "No. Our school system has some 80 different languages. We can't possibly provide translation for everyone." The meeting concluded.

FAMILY VIEWS OF THE PLACEMENT CONFERENCE

Although Clementina's mother and aunt did not understand everything that had transpired at Clementina's placement conference, they agreed with the multidisciplinary team's diagnosis. When we asked Rosa if she understood the term the staffing specialist had used during the staffing to describe Clementina, EMR, she said that she did not. Once it was explained that this meant that Clementina had mental limitations, but that she still could learn at school, the mother responded, "Yes, that is true." Her aunt added:

> Yes, she has those problems. . . . She has trouble in learning and also with her memory. . . . She runs a lot, without any reason, laughing and talking nonsense all the time. I was recommending that she [Rosa] should take the girl to see a doctor. I have one grandson who was declared disabled and is under special care. The school evaluated him, the same as Clementina has been, and told me what to do. Right now he is attending special classes. . . . The fact is that kids with this kind of mental trouble need to be under special care. She [Rosa] has to make an appointment with the doctor to take Clementina to the pediatrician so he can refer her to some of these places that give this kind of support. That is where I am taking my grandson, and there you learn how to take care of them. If the school gives you a paper so you can take them to the doctor, then you can get this kind of help.

SPECIAL EDUCATION PLACEMENT

Clementina seemed more comfortable and confident in her new self-contained EMR class than she had been in her general education classrooms. Her attendance improved. Her special education teacher believed that she had been appropriately placed, although she was functioning at a higher level than indicated by her test scores. She shared:

> Clementina is one of the smartest in her group. . . . Clementina is a good fit. She will catch up. She's in the fourth grade and for her to be just placed in a program is very sad. She has lost a lot of time. But she doesn't have [bad] behavior. She should catch up by her sixth-grade year. . . . She's not as low as they said. However, she is in math. She reads a lot more words, not just *dog*. She's like at a pre-primer level. In fact, she's in my middle group and she's the smartest one in that group. I tried putting her in the high group, but it was too hard for her.

Her mother was also pleased, noting that she was doing better than previously and liked her new class. She noted, "She gets up earlier and faster. You can tell that she wants to go to school."

Questions

1. Clementina's teachers and family did not disagree with the decision of the multidisciplinary team that Clementina was EMR. So perhaps we should conclude, "All's well that ends well." Discuss whether we have an accurate picture of Clementina's potential and of her strengths and learning needs.
2. How was Clementina affected by not being placed in special education until the end of fourth grade although she was originally referred in kindergarten?
3. Review your local school district's publication describing parents' procedural safeguards. From what you have read, what procedural safeguards were violated in Clementina's case? How might this have affected the outcome?
4. Review the definition for MR. Assessments should include an adaptive-behavior scale, which was omitted in this evaluation. Why do you think this is a requirement for this classification? What potentially valuable information was omitted that would have painted a more complete picture of Clementina's overall functioning, at home as well as at school?
5. Pretend that you are a parent advocate who was contacted to represent Clementina's family at her CST meeting and placement conference. What issues of concern would you raise? Don't forget to address issues related to her family's native language.

CHAPTER 10

Educable Mentally Retarded, English-Language Learner, or Ignored?

Bartholomew: *"so?"*

> I give Bartholomew the flash card with the word, "so." He reads it correctly. I ask him what it means. He replies, "So?" with an expressive shrug. I ask him to tell me in other words what it means and he replies, "I don't care!" (Researcher's observation notes)

Bartholomew had a history of having traveled back and forth from Haiti. He was in the third grade at Palm Grove Elementary School, an inner-city school where the student population was predominantly of Haitian ethnicity. We did not have an opportunity to observe Bartholomew in his general education classroom, since the case came to our attention at the point of referral. Ms. Marble, his third-grade homeroom teacher, was a White veteran teacher with more than 30 years' teaching experience and a strict but lively teaching style. She described Bartholomew to us as follows:

> This is a very sweet and innocent little boy who is so far behind that it's impossible to catch up. He doesn't know his alphabet. He doesn't know the sounds. He knows numbers. He can't add and subtract single digits. I mean, he's just way, way, way . . . Um . . . He's way off somewhere, but sweet. He's going to fourth grade. He can't do anything. If they don't hurry up, he'll be in middle school not being able to do anything.

EDUCABLE MENTALLY RETARDED

Bartholomew was tested and found eligible for services under the category EMR, with a secondary disability of speech impairment. Ms. Marble expressed doubts about the validity of the IQ testing because she felt "pretty sure" that he should have qualified for "trainable retarded," rather than "educable." She was of the impression that the Haitian psychologist had used a "softer" IQ test that inflated his IQ so as to qualify him for the higher category. This belief was dispelled, however, at the placement conference.

Present at the conference were Mr. St. Louis, Bartholomew's father; Mr. Pierre, the school's Haitian community liaison/translator; Ms. Marble, the referring teacher; Ms. Bolanos, the receiving special education teacher at the school to which Bartholomew was to be sent; and Ms. Martin, Palm Grove's ESOL teacher. Dr. Hall, Palm Grove's regular psychologist, presented the report on behalf of the Haitian psychologist who had done the testing.

Dr. Hall reported that Bartholomew earned a composite score of 55 on the Kauffman (K-ABC), a well-respected test commonly used by psychologists in the district. Bartholomew's reading was reported to be at the kindergarten level and his math at first grade. On the Scales of Independent Behavior (SIB), Bartholomew was found to have "limited to very limited" adaptive functioning. The report also noted that the psychologist gave Bartholomew directions in both Haitian Creole and English, and that his severe stuttering made it difficult to assess his verbal abilities. Dr. Hall, however, commented that Bartholomew had scored low on both verbal and nonverbal tasks. He concluded that Bartholomew scored in the "mentally deficient or close to trainable range," and was, "essentially, a third grader functioning at a K–1 level in all areas of academic skills."

Bartholomew was placed in a self-contained class at a nearby school, in which there would be small numbers and a paraprofessional to assist the teacher. The goals noted on his IEP focused on improvement in vocabulary development, word-study skills, writing skills through copying words, visual motor coordination, and using manipulatives to count to 10. Bartholomew would also receive speech therapy twice weekly.

PLACEMENT IN THE LEAST RESTRICTIVE ENVIRONMENT

There was one controversial issue discussed in this conference—whether Bartholomew should continue to participate in a program known as Home Language Arts (HLA), also known as Bilingual Curriculum Content (BCC). The school district required that eligible children be given access to this program, in order to help them maintain and develop their native language. When Ms. Martin, the ESOL teacher, made this suggestion, the special education teacher, Ms. Bolanos, exclaimed forcefully, "All my kids are self-contained, they don't go out." Ms. Martin reiterated that all students at ESOL Levels 1–4 were supposed to receive HLA. Ms. Bolanos stated that she was endorsed in ESOL methods, seeming to suggest that the ESOL component would fulfill the HLA component (although ESOL strategies means teaching in English). Another team member interjected that the school district was getting very strict about this and that Bartholomew "needs his Creole." Nevertheless, the HLA program was not included in Bartholomew's IEP.

Bartholomew's father, in a reserved and polite manner, expressed agreement that his son was very much behind. He said, several times, that the school should go ahead and do "whatever is good for him." He agreed readily to all decisions and asked eagerly when the services would begin. He did not comment on the HLA discussion and his opinion was not invited.

SPECIAL EDUCATION: "MY CHILDREN DON'T GO OUT"

We began observations of Bartholomew in his new school about 6 weeks after his placement. There were about 12 children in the class, about 7 of whom were boys and the majority of whom were Black—some Haitian, some African American.

Our observations corroborated Ms. Marble's impressions of Bartholomew's personality and achievement levels. However, we were also of the impression that the quick intelligence evident in the leading quote of this story could easily be obscured by Bartholomew's extreme shyness and soft speech, his severe stutter, and his limited English-language skills. Bartholomew's communication difficulties were evident in our observation notes. Ms. Bolanos, his special education teacher, had great difficulty understanding much of what he said to her, as is illustrated in the following observation of a writing task during the Thanksgiving season:

> Joanne, the girl next to Bartholomew, is to write the sentences that he will dictate . . . copying from the board the sentence "I am thankful" and filling in what Bartholomew tells her. He dictates his sentences in a very soft, childish voice and I have to listen very carefully to hear him. . . . Bartholomew says, "I love to go BCC." The teacher comes by at that point and I tell her what he said. She says that he does not go to BCC here because "Bartholomew cannot handle going out to another class. He needs to stay here with me. . . . It's nice to keep the home language but sometimes 'something's got to give' and since he's living in the U.S. now, English is what he needs." She then goes on to say that her philosophy is that everyone has a strength and that's what she works on to make sure that these children develop some confidence in one area. In Bartholomew's case, it's math, since his reading is very low. She thinks the most important thing is to build up his math skills. Then she'll move on to more of a focus on reading.

She moves away and Joanne asks Bartholomew what to write. He says again, "I love to go to BCC." She writes, "I am thankful to go to BCC." She has to turn the paper over to finish the last three words. They have now finished all six items. Bartholomew gets up and takes his paper to the teacher. She brings it back to the desk and goes over the items. . . . She gets to the last sentence, which, on this page, reads, "I am thankful to" and the other side has "go to BCC." She thinks that the sentence is unfinished and tells him he could write "help my Dad." Bartholomew tells her, "The other side," but she does not understand and tells him, "No, I don't need to write on the other side. I can write it here." And she writes, "help my Dad." He says again, "No, over here." But she either doesn't hear him or doesn't understand. I say, "He's telling you that the sentence is finished on the other side." She says, "Oh!" and turns over. She looks at the words "go to BCC" and it seems the meaning does not register on her. She turns back and is about to ignore it all. I say, "they've written, 'go to BCC.'" She turns the page again and says, "Oh, to go to BCC? Oh, OK." Then she reiterates that it's nice that he used to go at his other school but he can't here.

PROGRESSING IN MATH

Bartholomew worked hard at his math. During one observation in November, we found some sheets of sums under his chair, but none of the sums had check marks. He may not have been very well organized, since, upon seeing the sheets, Ms. Bolanos expressed surprise and commented that Bartholomew had never turned them in. She told him that he must turn in all his work. He did seem to be progressing in math: In October, he moved from addition and subtraction of numbers under 10, to addition of two digits, without regrouping (e.g., 25 + 11, 91 + 8), and subtraction of single digits from numbers up to 20 (e.g., 14 – 7). He would work on these laboriously, and his earlier sums were done by drawing the appropriate number of circles and crossing out as he subtracted. At the end of November, his work samples seldom showed the use of the circles strategy. In February, he was learning 2 and 5 times tables and, in May, Ms. Bolanos reported that he had begun to grasp the concept of regrouping.

There was much less evidence of progress in reading. In one visit, when we asked the teacher to tell us what Bartholomew was working on for reading, she turned to him and asked for the flash cards he had had for a month. Pulling about eight laminated cards out of his desk, Bartholomew told the teacher that the rest were "at home." She responded that he must bring them back, since he's only allowed to have them for home practice for a month. It was in reading these flash cards to us that Bartholomew gave us his memorable definition of "so?"

Midway through the year, we reminded Ms. Bolanos of the referring teacher's informal comment at the end of the placement conference, that Bartholomew would probably need to be reevaluated for a TMH (trainable mentally handicapped) placement in the subsequent year. Ms. Bolanos said, "He's definitely not trainable," saying that she felt he was appropriately placed and was making slow but steady progress in his work. She did not think it likely, however, that he would ever return to the general education mainstream.

Later in that year, we received disturbing news from Ms. Bolanos. She reported that Bartholomew seemed to be having signs of petit mal seizures and was about to undergo medical testing. We were not able to contact his father to investigate further, and unfortunately, we were left not knowing how this turn of events would affect Bartholomew.

Questions

1. What special difficulties do you feel arise in the classroom when a child has speech difficulties? What would you do as Bartholomew's teacher to help alleviate these difficulties?
2. When a child has multiple disabilities, how do you feel IEP goals can meet the needs of each disability? Pretend you are Bartholomew's special education teacher and create a series of goals and objectives for him based on what you know about his abilities at that time.
3. Some members of the team were concerned that part of Bartholomew's learning problems might have been related to the fact that his first language was not English. List all the examples from this case where this seemed to be an issue. Do you believe that Bartholomew should have continued to receive instruction in Creole for part of the day? What would have been the advantages and disadvantages?
4. Refer to the 2004 reauthorization of IDEA specifically as it pertains to the least restrictive environment. Do you believe that Bartholomew was being served in the least restrictive environment for him? In a group of four, debate the merits of segregated classes for students labeled EMR versus including these students in the general education classroom. Pair two people on each side of the issue.

CHAPTER 11

Learning Disabled or Absent?

Miles: *"I can add and subtract just like them."*

"A very bright, very charming child!" "A wonderful little boy! He has lots of girlfriends all around the school! His problems are in recognizing letters and beginning sounds of letters and answering questions." These were the descriptions given of Miles by, respectively, the psychologist who evaluated him and the kindergarten teacher who referred him. Always smartly dressed, Miles was also very handsome, with dark smooth skin and the face of a cherub. Perhaps even more endearing to the school personnel who worked with him were his unusually good manners for a kindergartner. His special education teacher exclaimed: "He's so lovable! So polite! He says, 'Yes, ma'am!'"

MS. MARTIN'S KINDERGARTEN CLASS

Miles first caught our attention as he worked alone on his math in Ms. Martin's kindergarten class. Ms. Martin was a Black woman who had been teaching at the school for about 13 years. Her classroom was one of the most peaceful places we had found in all our observations across the schools. When we asked her about her perceptions of the children at this predominantly African American inner-city school, she replied, "When you close the classroom doors, these children are no different from any other." Our notes of that day illustrate the excellent climate and structure of this teacher's class:

> There are children sitting in clusters around three tables. There are five or six at the table with Ms. Martin, working on adding with plastic counters. On the mat at the back of the room are three or four children sitting, playing cards. . . . There are about four at the house-keeping corner and one alone at a desk, with a woman [paraprofessional] working with Ms. Martin. After a while, some children move to other centers, such as two girls on the mat who choose books and

look at them together. . . . Occasionally, Ms. Martin quietly says things like, "I like the way Shaniqua is sitting quietly," or "Please do your work," or "There are too many girls at housekeeping." The children respond appropriately to all these comments. There is a boy alone at a desk working on some sums.

MILES'S FIRST YEAR IN KINDERGARTEN

The boy seated alone was Miles, whom Ms. Martin had told us she was worried about because his academics were so low. She believed that he did not know his numbers. Miles was working on a sheet of simple subtractions under 6. He had filled out almost the entire sheet, but all his answers were wrong. It only took a few questions to discover that he didn't realize he was supposed to be subtracting. When asked what the minus sign meant, he asked, "To write a word?" "More?" After explaining that it meant to take some away, we then noticed that he did not have the idea of starting at the top of the sum and then taking away what is below. In demonstrating the concept using his fingers, he seemed to get the idea quickly but got mixed up with how to put his fingers up. Yet he seemed to have the concept of zero quite well, answering correctly to "You have three cookies and I take away zero, what do you have left?" and also to "You have one and I take it away, how many do you have?" He exclaimed "Zero!" with great gusto. After walking him through several sums we told him to do some more on his own, but he got them all wrong again. Yet when we suggested that maybe he had done enough for the day he pointed to a new row and asked if they were right. When told no, he insisted that we must show him how to do them over. This time we used plastic counters and the lesson went much better, with Miles sometimes miscounting but showing that he was getting the idea. We noticed, too, that he was confusing the numerals 4 and 5.

REFERRAL AND EVALUATION

It turned out that the reason Ms. Martin was unsure of Miles's skills was that he was very often absent. She did refer him for evaluation, and at his CST meeting in April, his attendance record indicated 28 absences, mainly in the earlier part of the school year. His mother, Marie, said that Miles's asthma was the main reason for his poor attendance. However, she expressed great concern about his delayed progress in his schoolwork and some aspects of his development, saying, "He's not doing what a 5-year-old should. He can't even tie his shoes."

The psychologist reported Miles's assessment outcome as a clear profile of LD. On the WISC III, Miles' composite score was 90, with a performance score of 80 and a verbal score of 101. A test of visual motor skills indicated a deficit. When the psychologist reported that Miles was very creative and imaginative, his mother agreed, saying that he loved to tell stories and that he could be very entertaining. The psychologist concluded her report with the recommendation that Miles be placed in the primary special education class on a part-time basis, since he was "too smart" to need a full-time placement. The team agreed that, because his academics were so far behind, Miles should be retained in kindergarten in addition to his special education placement.

REPEATING KINDERGARTEN AND WORKING HARD IN SPECIAL EDUCATION

In the fall of that year, Miles's homeroom was a kindergarten class taught by Ms. Mallory, a Black woman. Most of our observations of him were done in his 12-hour-per-week primary special education class taught by a Hispanic teacher, Ms. Perez, whose gentle but firm manner was very supportive to her students. Her class initially included 16 K–3 students designated as having LD, who came to her throughout the day for math, reading, or both. Ms. Perez also had a paraprofessional in her room for 1½ hours in the mornings. The number of students in this class grew throughout the year, with Ms. Perez's official load rising to 24 at one point. There was one month, however, when Ms. Perez was required to teach all 42 students receiving special education services, because of the resignation of the intermediate special education teacher and the difficulty in finding a replacement for her.

Ms. Perez had high expectations for her LD students. For example, her first graders completed second-grade math before the end of the year, adding and subtracting three digits with regrouping. She felt that their problems were not so much related to math as to attention difficulties in a large group and to weak reading skills that made word problems difficult for them. She described most of her students as being "close to grade level," often with weak writing skills, and her goal was to have them all on grade level by the end of the year.

In describing her approach, Ms. Perez she said that although she looks at the psychological report, she assumes they know nothing and "starts from scratch." She emphasized, "I give them time. I don't rush them. I ask for quality, not quantity, of work." Most of these students, she said, lacked confidence and "think they're dumb." So she would tell them, "No, you're smart! Because to be in this class, you have to score high enough in IQ."

Then she would explain to them that they just have to work hard to improve their reading or whichever area was weak.

We began observing Miles in his special education placement at the end of September. Ms. Perez reported that he was consistently focused and attentive, always wanting "things to be done just right." He worked independently on the computer, including being able to log on and enter his own code. We watched as he got 18 out of 24 items correct in a task of selecting the "different" item, some of which were phonics related, such as selecting a picture of a house as not beginning with a *p* as did *pencil* and *pail*.

On finishing his computer tasks, Miles went directly to join three other boys at a table where they would work on math. He quickly offered to get crayons, glue, scissors, and pencils for the table, and Ms. Perez exclaimed, "I'm so happy with my helper today." When given sheets with basic shapes, Miles correctly identified the rectangle and counted the number of squares, while the older boys worked on math sums. At one point, Miles leaned close to the researcher sitting next to him and, pointing to the older boys, whispered, "I can add and subtract like them, but they put me back in kindergarten."

About 2 weeks later, it seemed that Ms. Perez had come to agree with Miles's assessment of his readiness for math. Telling us that "he's doing well," she explained that at first she had him doing shapes and colors, but having discovered that "he can do much more," she had moved him on to adding and subtracting.

By mid-October, it was evident that Miles was progressing quickly on all his IEP goals. In math, although his IEP goal was a kindergarten goal, to know the numbers 1–20 and match them to corresponding objects, Ms. Perez had started him on a first-grade math book. His work revealed that he had grasped the concepts of 1:1 correspondence and of more and fewer. He knew the numbers 1–7, but tended to forget 8 and 9. Using pictures, he would correctly add 3 + 1, 1 + 1 and so on. Ms. Perez anticipated that he would have mastered the 1–20 goal by Christmas and would be ready to move on to a first-grade goal of 1–50. Upon his completion of these goals she would call an interim IEP meeting with the kindergarten teacher and the parent to set new goals.

In pre-reading, Miles moved quickly from sequentially ordering two pictures to ordering four, which was his goal. He knew the letters A through K and could write them correctly and quite neatly both in upper- and lowercase. He also knew his colors and shapes. All Miles's work was very neat, his pictures carefully colored within the lines. Ms. Perez was about to begin pre-primer sight words with him and had arranged her schedule so as to be able to work on reading with Miles and the other kindergartner separately from the older students.

One area of Miles's IEP that was clearly incongruous covered the goals for behavior and social communication. Ms. Perez was so surprised at them that she wondered if the teacher had been absent at the July placement meeting. For example, the goals included "improve school behavior, follow one-step directions, complete task, seek assistance when necessary, improve communication skills," and "participate in group activities." Miles's behavior, in fact, was exemplary, and he was very helpful to another boy who was very quick tempered. Miles would tell his friend to "calm down" when he was getting upset.

By October, Ms. Perez had concluded that Miles's difficulties in the previous year may have been the result of frequent absences. She commented, "I'll keep an eye on him; maybe he needs to be mainstreamed." When we asked if it would be possible to rescind the retention and move him up if he progressed quickly to first-grade level, Ms. Perez said it would be possible, but more likely that he would remain in kindergarten and she could move him on to first-grade goals. She exclaimed, "That's the beauty of the program! The flexibility." With regard to mainstreaming, she was of the opinion that "by next year he can be partially mainstreamed."

Miles's performance in his repeat kindergarten class was also very good. We observed him writing his letters well; taking his time; and when he finished ahead of the others, turning over his paper and continuing to write his name.

A notable feature of Miles's development was his impressive vocabulary. We observed him volunteering such words as *community*, and explaining to his peers that a mail carrier's job is to "deliver the mail." In one conversation about animals, the teacher asked for examples of animals they could see in the zoo. Some children suggested tiger, lion, and zebra. Miles suggested "otter" and "sea lion."

At the end of the school year, Ms. Perez was very pleased with Miles's progress. His attendance had been very good and his improvement steady. He was then adding single digits up to 20 and he knew all the letters of the alphabet and sight words at the primer level. Ms. Perez concluded that Miles was certainly ready for first-grade reading and math. She planned to recommend that he be mainstreamed for reading. She wanted to keep him in her program for math, however, so that "if he needed extra help, he could benefit from this program."

MILES AT HOME

We paid one visit to Miles's home and learned quickly the source of his large vocabulary. Despite very cramped living quarters, Miles's mother, Marie, did all she could to create family activities for her two children. One such activity was a regular family night in which everyone watched the Discovery channel together and talked about it. Marie described Miles as "intelligent and imaginative." In listening to her we learned about a side of Miles we had not had the opportunity to see in our classroom observations. She said that he loved to act out different characters, "not just people he's seen on TV, but he even will act just like a doctor or a teacher, and talks like them and all. He's a scream!"

Marie was very concerned about Miles's difficulties in school and sought information from us about what might have caused his LD. She said that her meeting with the school team had not really explained anything about his disability but just that Miles would be "in the program." She wondered if his premature birth might be a factor, since he had weighed only 3 pounds and was late walking and talking. We advised her to seek advice from the school regarding sources of more analysis of Miles's development.

When we complimented Marie on her son's behavior and general demeanor, she said, "Yes, he's very well mannered. He's an easy child to raise—gives me no trouble and it seems like everyone at the school knows him and likes him." She asked us if we thought that Miles "really needed the program." She went on to say, "I wouldn't like him to be kept back for no reason but I do agree that he's having trouble." We replied that we thought his kindergarten teacher would not have recommended this if she didn't think he really needed it. Marie agreed, saying, "Yes, she's a good teacher."

Questions

1. The No Child Left Behind Act requires that students no longer be "socially promoted" or moved up to the following grade level until they are on grade level. What do you think of the decision to retain Miles in kindergarten while also providing special education services? What are the implications for special education students, who are by definition not performing on grade level?

2. Review the current definition of *specific learning disabilities*. What do you believe to be the causes of Miles's learning difficulties? Do you consider Miles to be a student with a disability?

3. Do you think when a student is a "borderline" case for needing special education services that it is better to keep the student in a general education or a special education setting? Make a list of the pros and cons of each setting and share your list with a partner.

4. Parent involvement has been shown to be an important factor in the educational outcome for students, particularly those living in inner cities. However, the notion of "involvement" may mean different things for different families. In Miles's case, is there anything teachers could have done to build on his mother's efforts? Go online and research ways that schools can create positive relationships with parents in inner-city neighborhoods.

CHAPTER 12

Learning Disabled
or Absent?

Anita: *"I'm tired of this school and all their mistakes!"*

'Cause they complain to me, 'You're not sending her to school, she's not getting an education.' So I send her to school. Guess what! She still don't get it. (Anita's mother)

Mabel Oakes, a full-service school, rests* in the northwestern corner of one of the poorest communities in the United States. This community is made up of African Americans, who have lived in the area for several generations, some Haitian immigrants and migrant farmworkers, who have only in the past decade begun to live in the area on a seasonal basis. Several Mexican families have "settled out," making the community their permanent home. Anita's family structure was somewhat unique in that her mother was Anglo-American from the Appalachian region, while her father was a Mexican migrant farmworker who lived nearby, in a separate house. Anita's mother, Ms. Volts, described herself as a "hillbilly" who did not complete high school. School personnel believed that Anita's mother had mental retardation. Upon our meeting and talking to Ms. Volts, her insights into her daughter's education and her sharp ability to understand the dynamics of her community counteracted this belief. According to Ms. Volts, she suffered from anxiety and depression and during her school years had been in a class for "crazy dumb people."

All three counselors from the school frequently cited problems with Ms. Volts. Stating that she was "against the school," they advised us that if we wanted to gain entrée to the family for our research, we should find a different way to get in touch with her, rather than aligning ourselves with the school. The full-service coordinator, a Hispanic female, told us that the school was having a lot of trouble with Ms. Volts because she spoke out at

---

*Authors' note: This chapter was written by Elizabeth Cramer and Keith Sturges.

parent meetings saying that the school was not addressing her daughter's needs. A Black counselor, Ms. Finn, told us that Ms. Volts had requested Anita be switched to a different class when she was having trouble the first time around in first grade. According to Ms. Finn, Anita's mother believed that Anita and her original first-grade teacher had different ways of communicating and Anita could not understand her. Ms. Finn expressed the opinion that this problem was one of cultural difference, since the original first-grade teacher was Black. Ms. Finn went on to say that Anita's mother "had some sort of mental problem," and added, "You can see it in her face."

FIRST GRADE: SECOND TIME AROUND

We met Anita at the beginning of her 2nd year in the first grade. She had been retained the previous year. The reason that Anita was viewed as a concern to her teacher, Mrs. Applebaum, was her poor attendance and apparent lack of attention during class. Ms. Applebaum, a Jewish American woman, kept her class generally engaged and fairly well behaved. In one of our classroom observations we recorded that Anita was being disruptive during story time, but for the most part, Anita was not even noted during observations because she was often absent, and when present, she was usually sitting quietly in the room.

The school social worker and counselor had pointed Anita out as a prospective target student for our research because they thought her family would make an interesting case for study. Our researcher's field notes reported not having noted Anita, since she seemed to stay on task and get along with her friends.

The official reason appearing on Anita's referral to special education was poor attendance. After Anita was evaluated, the reason given on the multidisciplinary-team report was poor academic progress. The teacher's reports for the evaluation revealed that Anita did not complete tasks, had a short attention span, was easily distracted, daydreamed, and seemed to have difficulty staying in her seat. The reports also noted her lack of enthusiasm, self-confidence, and motivation. Anita was tested for IQ, achievement, processing, and emotional adaptation using, respectively, the WISC III; the Woodcock Johnson Tests of Achievement, revised edition; the Bender Visual Motor Gestalt Test; the Beery-Buktenica Development Test of Visual Motor Integration; the House-Tree-Person Test; the Kinetic Family Drawing; and a clinical interview. Anita scored within the average range on all IQ measures (verbal IQ of 80, performance IQ of 93, and a full-scale IQ of 84) but below grade level on achievement measures. The assessors noted the discrepancies between her verbal and performance IQ scores as well as between her IQ score and achievement. Her visual motor skills were also found to be significantly underdeveloped for her age. She was found eligible for LD.

When we asked Ms. Applebaum about her decision to refer Anita, she stated that she originally planned to retain her but that this was not allowed because she had already been retained. She then described Anita:

> Academically, way behind everybody else. She has trouble with number concepts, she has trouble with reading, she has trouble with writing, she's just generally very poor. And it's obviously not a maturation problem, since she's already a year older than all the other children. She also has a very, very poor attendance record, which doesn't help. . . . Her mother claims that she has a variety of minor ailments, so we referred her.

SECOND GRADE: ABSENT AND INVISIBLE

In October the following year, Anita was placed in special education, receiving instruction in reading and math in Ms. Paritton's part-time resource class for students with LD. For the rest of her classes she remained in the general education second-grade classroom with Ms. Walters and her nondisabled peers.

Social Issues

According to her mother, Anita's absences were the result of a combination of several bouts with lice and pinkeye as well as Anita's appeal to her mother that she did not want to go to school. Anita told us that she did not like school because she wanted to play and did not get to play anymore since she was in second grade.

She had friends in the regular education class, and when she was there, she would talk with the other students at her table. During lunch and PE, she participated with other students from Ms. Walters's class and got along well. Most of the students in her class were off task and talking during instruction time in our observations and she was actually one of the better-behaved students in the room.

When we asked Anita how she felt about school, she replied that she used to like school in kindergarten but that she didn't like it anymore because they do "too much work." She stated that she liked Ms. Parriton's class better than Ms. Walters's general education class because Ms. Walters "gives too much work and screams at them." She said that she did not get along well with many of her classmates and felt lonely a lot. When questioned further, she said that some kids were mean and that they wanted to fight her and be mean to her. She stated that students had pushed her and hit her. She said that sometimes during PE students tried to beat her up. In our two observations of her PE class, we did not see these difficulties.

Anita's Work

Anita continued to perform below grade level in both reading and math. While writing from a prompt in the general education classroom, she asked how to spell just about every word she wrote. When told to sound out words, she was able to spell most of them either correctly or close to correctly. She did not have confidence in her ability to spell and wanted to check each word with a teacher. She also asked other students at her table area for assistance in spelling. Samples of her work show immature but clear handwriting with poorly developed language skills. On a worksheet with a rectangular frame, she wrote:

> Brid live and nest
> Thye have Feather
> To FlY and warm the eggs
> Brid hav mon in Dad
> They KeeP They eggs
> Warm i Save
> Wintiwind TheY KeeP
> The eggs warm
> When I Write I Should
> AlWays make it neat. MY
> Teacher will be happy and
> My WorK Willook Nice.

The special education class used the Success for All reading program. While reading aloud in the special education class, Anita read well. Although below grade level, she was one of the better readers in this class and moved quickly and accurately through her passages. When the other students read aloud, she played with her hair or items inside her desk and did not follow along.

General Education Class

In the general education class, Anita was often ignored and seemed to disappear into the background. In one observation, half the students were working on a tutorial program on the computers and the other half moved to one section of the room to sit in a circle and hear Ms. Walters read a story. Anita remained at her desk, staring into space. Halfway into the story, Ms. Walters looked up and saw her and told her she was welcome to join them if she wanted to do so. Ms. Walters, a White veteran teacher who had recently left teaching PE to teach second grade, acknowledged that she did not view Anita as her student once she was placed in special education. Many times during the course of the year the special education classes were canceled because of Ms. Parriton's absence. When this happened, Anita stayed with Ms. Walters all day. Since Ms. Walters did not normally teach Anita reading or math, she either did not give Anita anything to do or she gave her grade-level work that was far above her level and did not collect or grade it. When we observed Anita in the general education classroom Ms. Walters would make comments such as "Oh great, you can take her to the back and do reading," even though we had told her we were there only to observe.

During observations of Anita, it became clear that class routines that the other students were all familiar with were not routine for Anita. In one instance, the students took turns going to the computers to work on the Success for All program. When it was Anita's turn, she did not know how to log on. Halfway through the school year, this was an activity that took place each day and was second nature to the other students. In another observation, Ms. Walters placed a prompt on the board and all the students took out their journals and started writing. Anita sat at her desk for around 5 minutes staring straight ahead, then reached into her desk, opened her journal, and started flipping through the pages. Mrs. Walters told her to take her journal out. She did so and then looked at the closed cover. After a couple of minutes had passed, Anita went up to Ms. Walters and asked her what she was supposed to do. Ms. Walters pointed to the prompts, and Anita went back to her seat and began writing. During this time, all the other students had copied the prompt and written their entries. Her teachers attributed situations like this to the fact that she was absent so often that she never really got accustomed to all the little things that went on throughout the day.

Special Education Class

Ms. Parriton was a young Black woman whose special education classroom had a much more laid-back feeling to it than the general education classroom. Although she did raise her voice, she was speaking in a loud tone rather than yelling, as compared to Ms. Walters, who was often observed to be yelling at students.

Anita missed many special education classes because of absenteeism, but also because sometimes when she was at school she would forget to go to Ms. Parriton's class. During one observation Ms. Parriton was passing back old graded papers. Most students had at least five papers handed back to them. Anita did not get any papers back. Later Ms. Parriton passed back folders for the students to put their work into. Anita did not get a folder either and did not say anything to the teacher. We went to Ms. Parriton and asked if Anita had a folder. Ms. Parriton asked Anita if she had got a folder back and Anita said no. She asked if Anita had received any work back and again Anita said no. These folders were full of all the classwork and homework that students had done all year. Anita didn't have one. When we asked Ms. Parriton how this could be, she told us that Anita didn't turn in any work. She told us that Anita probably had a math folder and we were welcome to look through any of her work. We looked through all the boxes of folders. There were math folders, homework folders, reading folders, language arts folders, journal folders, and math workbooks. Each of the other students had each of these folders. Anita did have a math folder, in which there were three timed tests and one worksheet. On two of the tests she had done well, and on the other she had answered only the first 4 of 30 questions. Every item on the worksheet was wrong. All these items were basic one-digit addition and subtraction. This was the only work that Ms. Parriton had for Anita from the school year. This observation took place in February.

During a full-day observation, we observed Anita's math time. During the time that Ms. Parriton's class was scheduled to have math, the class was coloring. After the students finished coloring, Ms. Parriton gave the students a timed one-digit addition quiz. They had a few minutes to complete the quiz; those few minutes were the only minutes spent on math. During the quiz, Ms. Parriton walked around and stopped at Anita's desk and noted that she was subtracting. Ms. Parriton exclaimed, "Addition! Addition! Addition! Plus, plus, plus! Bigger numbers [gestures to indicate bigger]. Not subtraction, not take away. In other words, erase them, they're wrong. I'm trying to tell you." Anita did not seem to understand what Ms. Parriton was trying to say and kept completing them using subtraction. Ms. Parriton told her to use her fingers to count, but she got each answer wrong.

SOMEBODY DO THE MATH: SCHEDULING ISSUES

Ms. Parriton's schedule included a 30-minute period after math, during which all the students but three (including Anita) left for lunch each day. During this time, Ms. Parriton gave the three remaining students downtime, rather than providing additional instruction. Anita usually straightened up the room or played. After lunch, Anita returned to Ms. Walters's room and sat while the class worked on spelling, and then the students went to PE. The other students in Ms. Parriton's special education class came from other classes that had PE at times that didn't interfere with the afternoon math block, but Ms. Walters's class had PE in the afternoon. Since students could not miss PE or art to go to special education, Anita went to PE and did not return to Ms. Parriton's special education class for math as the other students did. As a result, she only received one half hour of math instruction daily. Additionally, between the canceling of special education classes, Anita simply forgetting to go to Ms. Parriton's room, or lack of instruction during scheduled math time, there were many days when Anita received no math instruction at all. According to her mother:

> Anita's the only one out of the entire class that has to go [to special education] so when it's time to go . . . she don't go. 'Cause Anita, sometimes she forgets. . . . Anita can't tell time. . . . So at 12:45, she don't know what time it is, so she can't tell Ms. Walters, "Well, I've got to go to Ms. Parriton's class." So, she misses that day of math. . . . And too, that they don't know how to fix the schedule so that she can go during Spanish or PE, but they're like—well, she can't miss them classes. But it's OK if she miss math. Now that's the main thing. They [future employers] don't look to see on your application if you went to PE. They want to know what you know in math. So, of course she gonna flunk math. She don't take it. 'Cause they complain to me, "You're not sending her to school, she's not getting an education." So I send her to school. Guess what! She still don't get it.

FAMILY PERSPECTIVES: "I'M TIRED OF MABEL OAKES AND ALL THEIR MISTAKES"

In an interview, Ms. Volts stated that she was glad that Anita was placed in special education because she knew that Anita was not able to read or spell. She remarked that she knew that Anita would need to be in special education for a while because "it's not like her IQ is going to go boom, through the roof, or something. Usually it basically stays about the same." She stated that the special education was not a problem as long as she finished high school. Also, she did not want Anita passing unless she was up to the grade level. Ms. Volts was upset that they did not retain Anita again because she didn't think she was ready to pass the first grade, since she could not read close to grade level.

Anita's mother did not think that the school was providing her daughter with an education and therefore saw nothing wrong with letting Anita stay home from school. One of her mother's growing concerns was that the special education classes were often canceled. "They got substitutes for all the other homeroom classes. Why is that class different? What is it? Are they trying to tell me that my daughter's education is not important?"

THE BEGINNING OF THE END

As the school year went on, Ms. Volts began to show up less and less at the weekly parent breakfasts. Anita's attendance continued to be a problem, and the school had reported the family to the authorities. A case was pending and Ms. Volts was informed by truancy patrol that she would go to jail if Anita did not start attending regularly.

In an interview with Ms. Volts in April, she revealed that she was no longer happy with Mabel Oakes Elementary and was planning to move to another part of Fernwood City and move Anita to West Homefront Elementary School. When I asked her why, she told me:

> They started getting all up in my business talking about truancy. . . . "Well, we'll call truancy tips to make an appointment so they can talk to you. Oh, we're only doing this to help you." I said, "Fine, don't help me. Huh, I don't need no help that bad." They're like, "Everything we do for you we're just trying to help you." Oh, please. Don't help me. 'Cause the help they're giving me gets me in trouble. I'm like, shoot, go help somebody else.

Regarding the transfer to another school, she stated:

> I'm telling you that I'm gonna transfer her to another school basically because the [special education] program here in this school sucks. It ain't no good. I said if the teacher's not there, the kid don't go to class. . . . So I said, fine, send me to [truancy patrol], and when we do, I'm gonna ask them, since they're the district attorney or whatever they are, why Anita's teacher's not here, why don't she go to class. Why don't she have a substitute. I doubt they'd know that. . . . They want to sit there and say I'm helping you, fine, I'm gonna help them too. I wanna know, all the other schools get substitutes, why this one don't and they supposed to have all this helping the community and all this. And I'm like, huh, they need to forget about the community for a little while and think about the students that's in the school. . . . So, I'm tired of Mabel Oakes and all their mistakes.

Questions

1. Consult the current definition for LD. What do you believe to be the causes of Anita's learning difficulties? Do you consider Anita to be a student with LD?
2. What are some strategies that you may have used as Anita's special education teacher to try to help her make progress? How would you coordinate responsibility between the general and special education teachers?
3. Pretend that you are a parent outreach professional at Mabel Oakes Elementary School and you have been assigned to work with Anita's family. Develop a plan to improve the relationship with the mother.
4. What responsibility does the school have for ensuring regular attendance of students? Find out what the policy is in your local school district regarding the allowed amount of absences per year for each student. What types of resources are in place at the local level to counteract student truancy?
5. Should parents have the option of choosing another school if they are unsatisfied with their child's education? Find out what the policy on choice is in your school district. Get in a group with three of your classmates and compare your views on this topic.

CHAPTER 13

Learning Disabled or Low Achiever?

Marc: *"He's a quiet person in class; he's just slow."*

I can't do this by myself! I need your parents to do their part. (Marc's 4th-grade teacher)

Marc was* an 8-year-old third grader from Jamaica. He had come to Florida as a toddler and had only attended school in the United States. He was tall for his age, almost too big to fit comfortably at his desk. Initially, Marc was not the focus of our investigations. Because of his mild demeanor, he was able to fly under the radar for quite some time—even our radar.

We characterized Marc as cooperative and quiet, interacting with peers only when appropriate to do so. He never seemed to let socializing interfere with his school responsibilities. He was well behaved and compliant, even in special-area classes, such as Spanish, where peers tended to play around. According to Marc's mother, "He has never had a behavior problem. He always has good grades in behavior." Beaming, she said he had won perfect-attendance awards every year. He came to school every day and did not disturb anyone, so no one seemed to notice that he was struggling, at least until third grade.

Marc lived with his mother, named Elena, and two older brothers in their 20s. According to Elena, her older sons made a decent living in vocational trades and served as the male images and role models in the family. The family had recently moved into their first house. Marc had no other relatives in the United States, but his godmother lived nearby and assisted with child care. Elena had received her schooling in Jamaica. She noted that "back home," teachers were stricter. She added that in Florida the "children ruled" and the classes were so loud that the students did not receive the attention needed. She thought that this maybe played a role in Marc's academic struggles, "because he is a quiet person in class. He is not like the other kids." She thought Ms. Ruiz was harder than Marc's previous teachers and that

---

*Authors' note: This chapter was written by Cassaundra Wimes.

Marc "was just slow." Overall, she thought his school, Clearwater Elementary, was very good.

Clearwater was a predominantly Black school with demographics that revealed a stark contrast to the predominantly Black inner-city schools we studied. The percentage of students receiving free or reduced-price lunch was much less. The surrounding community was made up of single-family homes rather than apartment buildings. However, the neighborhood was changing, and Clearwater had just become a Title I school, yet the climate of the school was more like that of schools in middle-income neighborhoods. We saw inspired instruction in many classrooms, involved parents, and a school that seemed to be doing a lot of things right.

MARC'S REFERRAL AND PLACEMENT

Marc was one of 10 students in his third-grade class referred to the CST by his teacher. Ms. Ruiz was Hispanic, from Cuba, and considered an excellent teacher, able to motivate students with humor and enthusiasm but with a reputation of being "not easy." She was concerned about Marc's low reading and writing skills, as well as mathematics to a lesser extent, but not his behavior. She said he was reading at a "primer, pre-primer level." Marc's grades during the third quarter of third grade, when he was referred, were D's in language arts, reading, and mathematics and C's in science and social studies, with a 2 for effort (on a scale of 1 to 3) and a C for conduct in each.

On his referral form under "observation of student behaviors," Ms. Ruiz wrote: "short attention span," "easily distracted," "feelings of inferiority." She referred Marc in March, and he was evaluated and placed in a part-time LD class early in his fourth-grade year, qualifying based on a discrepancy between his I.Q. score and low achievement. It seemed clear that he did meet these criteria. Ms. Ruiz had tried to "rush" his case, frustrated that he had not been referred previously. She stated that his second-grade teacher "never referred anyone to the [special education] program."

Marc seemed to make good progress in the fourth-grade special education class, earning A's. However, his results on the Woodcock Johnson in April of fourth grade (age 9 years, 11 months) showed that he was about 2 years behind in all areas but calculation, where he was a year ahead:

- letter-word identification: age equivalent = 7-6; grade equivalent = 2.1
- passage comprehension: age equivalent = 8-1; grade equivalent = 2.6
- calculation: age equivalent = 11-0; grade equivalent = 5.6
- applied problems: age equivalent = 7-11; grade equivalent = 2.3

Marc told us that he liked going to the LD class, and that he especially enjoyed using the computers. He explained that his schedule consisted of attending LD classes three times a day, in the morning and again after lunch, for reading and math. His mother was quite concerned about what he was missing in his general education class and thought it was difficult for him to juggle two classes. She voiced concern that Marc spent more time in one class than the other, so he missed "important stuff." We noted that in his fourth-grade general education class, he and the other two special education students were isolated from the other students, with their desks placed in the far northwest corner of the classroom.

Each of the following examples is from a different observation in his special and general education classes. Although the instruction in both classes was rather routine, Marc was consistently diligent in attempting to complete his work. The examples also show the higher standard expected in the general education class.

Special Education Class:
- The intern said, "Name some of the chores you do at home." He called on several students. Marc said, "I make my bed and wash dishes." The intern directed students to write about their chores in their journals, adding, "When I look at your journals I want to see transition words." Marc laid his head down on his desk and started writing in his journal.
- The following problems were on the board:
  $502 - 217 =$
  $701 - 427 =$
  $605 - 176 =$
  Marc was diligently working on the math problems, counting on his fingers.
- We examined Marc's work. He had completed his homework, and the teacher had already checked and corrected it. Now he was copying over his sentences. We noted some spelling errors, such as "shier" instead of *share* and "ask" instead of *asked*, and his writing wasn't very neat.

General Education Class:
- The teacher, Ms. Mays, yelled at Marc, "Where is your homework packet?" Marc looked down morosely. "I want to see you during art," she said sternly. . . . Marc found his homework, which was several ditto sheets stapled together. The teacher came over. "Did you do your homework? Boy, you going to make me hurt you." "I did it," Marc said. "Oh, you're too smart!" she exclaimed.

- Ms. Mays placed more problems on the board and called on students to answer them. As the students wrote the correct answer on the board, Marc made changes on his paper. When it was Marc's turn, he solved the equation $14324 - 12242 = 02082$. Someone said, "That's wrong." "No, that's right," Ms. Mays said.

PARENTAL INVOLVEMENT

Elena was actively involved in Clearwater's PTA and volunteered frequently at the school, assisting in fund-raising efforts and helping in the school library. She read at home with Marc and encouraged him to read more often. Although our perception was that she was an involved, caring parent, she drew disparaging remarks from Marc's teachers. When checking his homework, the special education teacher exclaimed loudly, in front of the class, "I don't understand that they don't get help. No one helps them. With my son, I look over his shoulder. It kills me!" On another occasion, his fourth-grade teacher admonished, "I don't know what's going on here. Your parents aren't going over this homework with you. I told you. I can't do this by myself. I need your parents to do their part."

Questions

1. Marc's second- and third-grade teachers typified two very different approaches to special education referrals. One teacher had a reputation for "never referring anyone," while the other teacher referred nearly a third of her class. What should be the role of school and district administrators in monitoring the referral process? What should reasonable guidelines be regarding criteria for referring students?
2. It seemed that Marc's good behavior may have allowed his academic needs to go undetected. We know that disruptive students are more likely to be referred by their teachers. What should be done to ensure that all students get the help they need in a timely manner? How might a response-to-intervention model, with regular progress monitoring, have helped Marc?
3. Pull-out programs can be challenging for elementary school students. Marc's schedule required several transitions during the course of single day. Is there another way Marc could have received special education support? With a partner, think of the factors that must be considered when determining which type of special education program to provide.
4. The research is clear on the positive impact of parent involvement. Mark's mother focused on making sure Marc was in school every day and was

well behaved. She read to him and volunteered at the school. Yet teachers believed she did not help enough with homework. What constitutes effective parent involvement? What are teachers' responsibilities for facilitating relationship with parents and communicating their expectations? In Marc's case, what might the school and teachers have done?

CHAPTER 14

Between the Cracks?

Taddeus: "He can fix anything!"

He can fix anything! (Mother)
He's on the moon! (Teacher)

Taddeus was an African American boy who was repeating the second grade at South Park Elementary School. He was in the same class as Robert and had recently been referred for special education but was found not eligible for services. Taddeus was always nattily dressed, wearing long, crisply ironed shorts and smart cotton shirts a couple of sizes too big, in the style of many urban youth. He had a wide, shy smile, and his stocky build gave our researcher the impression of a "miniature football player"

His teachers, Ms. Robinson and Ms. Lopez, were surprised at the outcome of the evaluation. Ms. Lopez exclaimed, "I don't know why he didn't qualify for special ed!" She was of the opinion that Taddeus really needed to repeat the grade again, since it "would not be fair to pass him on when he knows nothing." She concluded, "He's on the moon!" Ms. Lopez said she had heard that there were gangs at his home and his cousin was killed recently. Shrugging, she added that Taddeus's mother came to pay for him to go the dance but didn't show up at the scheduled CST meeting.

We paid one visit to Taddeus's home to seek his mother's permission for him to participate in our study. His mother, Marsha, welcomed us with a smile and talked openly about some of the difficulties her family had faced. Violence had certainly hurt her family, an older son and a niece having been "caught in crossfire" in separate incidents in the neighborhood. We met that son, a neat, polite young man who greeted us pleasantly on his way out of the house.

When Marsha spoke of Taddeus, she emphasized his strengths. Acknowledging that he was having trouble with his schoolwork, she stated that he was the first of her children to have had so much trouble. Pointing to a bike leaning against the wall in the hallway, she exclaimed, "He can fix anything! People in the neighborhood pay him to fix bikes and things! My older son can't fix anything. Some people have trouble one way and others have something different."

When we talked with Taddeus, he told us that he found reading "hard," but he was good at math. His grade book showed social studies: CCCC; math: BBFD; math homework: 0000; language arts homework: 0000. Apparently he did no homework.

A quick test of addition and subtraction showed that he understood the concepts well and could do some simple additions in his head but relied a lot on his fingers. For such sums as 20 + 2, 30 + 6, or 100 + 5, he would answer correctly automatically without having to check. When asked 49 − 3, he raised his eyebrows and hesitated, then counted silently and said, "46."

In trying to assess his skills more closely, we sat with him for about a half hour as he worked on the schoolwide computer program that was individualized to each child's level. The first task was computing the time. The prompts used a clock face and it was evident that Taddeus had no trouble reading the time. Our field notes read:

> *The clock face says 50 minutes after 6. What time was it 9 hours and 20 minutes ago? Set the clock to show your answer.* Taddeus does not know what to do. I walk him through it and he seems to understand the process. I go over about two more with him and then he works out the next two on his own, slowly, but correctly.

The next task is a series of sums. He gets the first two correct on his own:

8 + 5 + ? = 18?
[He inserts 5]
90 − 3 = 87

He has more trouble with the next one:

w + 1 + 7 = 17; w = ?
[He hesitates. I ask him, 7 + 1? He says 8. I ask him how much more for 17. He counts up to 17 and writes in 9 as the answer.]

He correctly answers the next sums quickly without using his fingers:

10 − 3
9 − 1
11 − 2
6 − 6
11 − 8
7 − 0

For the next two, he looks at his fingers and answers correctly:

10 – 9
9 – 7

Next, the computer presents more clock face tasks:

[He is presented the following problem:] The time on the clock shows
5 minutes after 4 o'clock. What time will it be in 5 hours and 20
minutes?
[Taddeus starts by subtracting, as he had done for the previous ones. I
ask him if "will be" means later or before. He says, "Later." I ask
what he'll do. He says, "Add the hours: 5 and 4." I ask, "Then for the
minutes? 20 + 5?" He says, "29?" I prompt him to add by 5s. He says,
"25." Then he goes back and adds the 5 and 4 (hours) and says, "9."
Then he says, "9.25." He goes on to work out the next problem on his
own: 1.15 + 4 hours and 30 minutes = 5.45. It seems he now under-
stands the process but gets confused in adding the hours.]

Then he has to add money:

$3.30 + 1.10 = $4.40
1.20 + 2.20 = 3.40
[He points with his fingers but doesn't really count on them. He
seems to be doing these more in his head.]
$3.30 – 2.10 =
[He uses his fingers for this and says, "30 cents take away 10 cents,"
hesitates, then says, "20. One dollar and twenty cents."]

This brief exercise with Taddeus taught us a lot about his math skills.
First, he understood the processes involved in adding and subtracting but
did not have mental mastery of the facts. Second, despite the lack of mental
mastery, he seemed to figure out the arithmetic most quickly when it was
related to money. Third, he understood the verbal concepts, such as "later/
earlier," involved in estimating time. Fourth, he learned what was being
explained to him. Fifth, he needed someone to go through the tasks with him
and teach him the processes.
Taddeus was the kind of student that the principal of this school would
refer to as her "PDKs—pretty dumb kids":

These are the children who don't fit any label. . . . And if you cannot
wear a title, we put you nowhere and you get left out. . . . These are

the kids that are going to be taking care of us, cooking for us, servicing our vehicles, waiting on us in the hospitals or whatever. . . . These are the kids where you have to look for the talent and you develop that talent. By the time the child leaves elementary school you need to know what it is they like, what they excel in. . . . So what do you do? You can't retain a child that academically is never going to give you what you want because they are incapable of that. . . . A PDK could be self-sufficient, could read, could take care of business, could survive. But I think that up to now we have basically thrown them away. Right now, it's like there's one big track and everyone is on that track. But the PDKs can't fit that track because when their train stops, they are not getting off at college.

Questions

1. Do you feel that Taddeus has a disability? If so, what disability do you believe he has?
2. What does our information on Taddeus's math skills tell us about the instruction he has received? Seek information on current approaches to the teaching of arithmetic—for example, having children memorize the basic math facts.
3. Could knowing about Taddeus's talent in fixing things help? Pretend you are Taddeus's math teacher and you want to use his strengths to help him improve in math. Design an activity suited to his strengths to help him learn any of the specific concepts described in the case.
4. To what extent do you agree with the principal's PDK statement? Should students who fit this profile be eligible for special education instruction?

The Tyranny of the Norm

Our educational system is tyrannized by norms. The overwhelming emphasis on whether all children measure up to standardized models of development and learning creates a false view of "normalcy." The dominance of norms results in the belief that to be different is to be abnormal or, at least, deficient. The norms, however, are based on the levels of academic readiness manifested by children who have grown up in homes and neighborhoods that match school expectations. The fact is that children do not experience an equal playing field in terms of preparation for school. Nor do they experience an equal playing field when they enter school, since poor neighborhoods tend to get poor schools (Darling-Hammond & Post, 2000). Imposing the same set of norms on all children is patently unfair.

The tyranny of the norm can also be interpreted through the concept of "hegemony" (Gramsci, 1971), described as the overpowering influence of certain beliefs, practices, and values in a society. Thus, it is often said that racial, cultural, and social class power are hegemonic in our society: They are infused, sometimes invisibly, throughout our society's structures, and affect housing, health care, employment opportunities, and education. Many of the cases presented in this book illustrate the hegemony of these factors.

In education, the focus on normative rates of mastery of academic and behavioral standards adds yet another type of hegemony. That is, the education system applies middle-class learning and behavioral norms to all children, regardless of whether children have had opportunities to attain those norms. Normative measures then come to be seen as indicators of healthy functioning, and those who do not meet those norms are at increased risk of being seen as "disabled."

We offer these case studies as examples of how the excellent intentions of the special education system have been distorted to produce the impression that children from minority groups, who are mostly non-White and of diverse cultural and linguistic heritages, are disproportionately "disabled." We urge our readers to rethink the assumptions of the concept of disability and to consider how our society could better serve children with diverse needs and abilities.

References

Darling-Hammond, L., & Post, L. (2000). Inequality in teaching and schooling: Supporting high quality teaching and leadership in low income schools. In R. D. Kahlenberg (Ed.), *A notion at risk: Preserving public education as an engine for social mobility* (pp. 127–168). New York: The Century Foundation Press.

Donovan, S., & Cross, C. (2002). *Minority students in special and gifted education.* Washington, DC: National Academy Press.

Gramsci, A. (1971). *Selections from the prison notebooks.* (Q. Hoare & G. Nowell Smith, Eds. and Trans.). New York: International Publishers.

Harry, B., & Klingner, J. (2006). *Why are so many minority students in special education? Understanding race and disability in schools.* New York: Teachers College Press.

Harry, B., Klingner, J., & Hart, J. (2005). African American families under fire: Ethnographic views of family strengths. *Remedial and Special Education, 26*(2), 101–112.

Hart, J. E. (2003). *African American learners and 6-hour emotional disturbance: Investigating the roles of context, perception, and worldview, in the over-representation phenomenon.* Unpublished doctoral dissertation, University of Miami, FL.

Hosp, J. L., & Reschly, D. J. (2002). Regional differences in school psychology practice. *School Psychology Review, 31,* 11–29.

MacMillan, D. L., & Reschly, D. J. (1996). Issues of definition and classification. In W. MacLean (Ed.), *Handbook of mental deficiency: Psychological theory and research* (3rd ed.). Hillsdale, NJ: Lawrence Erlbaum.

Mercer, C. D., King-Sears, P., & Mercer, A. R. (1990). Learning disabilities definitions and criteria used by state education departments. *Learning Disability Quarterly, 13,* 141–152.

Public Law 108-446. (2004, December 3). *Individuals with Disabilities Education Improvement Act of 2004.* Congressional Record, H.R. 1350.

Serpell, R., Mariga, L., & Harvey, K. (1993). Mental retardation in African countries: Conceptualization, services, and research. *International Review of Research in Mental Retardation, 19,* 1–39.

U.S. Department of Education: Office for Civil Rights. (1999). *1997 Elementary and secondary school civil rights survey: National summaries.* Washington, DC: DBS Corporation.

U.S. Department of Education: Office of Special Education Programs. (2000). *Twenty-Second annual report to Congress on the implementation of the Individuals with Disabilities Education Improvement Act*. Washington, DC: Author.

U.S. Department of Education: Office of Special Education Programs. (2004). *Twenty-Sixth annual report to Congress on the implementation of the Individuals with Disabilities Education Improvement Act*. Washington, DC: Author.

U.S. Office of Education. (1977). Assistance to states for education for handicapped children: Procedures for evaluating specific learning disabilities. *Federal Register, 42*, 65082–65085.

Vaughn, S., & Fuchs, L. (2003). Redefining learning disabilities as inadequate response to instruction: The promise and potential problems. *Learning Disabilities: Research and Practice, 18*, 137–146.

Index

Academic issues
  and ADHD, 25, 26, 72, 77
  and attendance, 102
  and EBD, 25, 26, 40, 41, 43, 48, 49,
    50, 53, 54, 55, 56–60, 62, 63,
    68–69
  and EH, 72, 77
  and ELL, 62, 63, 68–69, 83–84, 85,
    87, 88, 89, 90–91
  and EMR, 11, 83–84, 85, 87, 88,
    89, 90–91
  and falling between the cracks, 114–
    15, 116
  and LD, 11, 13, 14, 40, 41, 43, 48,
    49, 50, 53–60, 62, 63, 68–69,
    72, 77, 93, 94, 95, 100, 101,
    102, 104, 105, 109, 111
  and norms, 117
  and referrals, 5
  See also IQ
Accountability, 71, 82
Adaptive functioning, 10
Adaptive-behavior scale, 84
ADHD (attention deficit hyperactivity
    disorder)
  and academic issues, 25, 26, 72, 77
  assessment of, 24, 25, 26, 71, 75,
    76–77
  and behavior, 22, 23, 24–25, 26, 28,
    72–74, 75
  case studies about, 21–28, 71–78
  as category of disability, 3–4
  definition of, 28, 78
  and EBD, 15, 21–28

  and EH, 71–78
  and ELL, 78
  and instruction, 22, 23
  and IQ, 25, 77
  and LD, 15, 71–78
  placement for, 24, 25–26, 27, 28,
    71–72, 75, 76–78
  questions about, 28, 78
  and race/ethnicity, 22, 28
  referral for, 71, 72, 74–75, 77
  and retention/promotion, 22, 24
  and tests, 76–77
American Association on Mental
    Retardation (AAMR), 9
Anita (case study), 99–107
Assessment/evaluation
  of ADHD, 24, 25, 26, 71, 75, 76–
    77
  and behavior, 16
  dilemmas of, 10, 12–14, 16–17
  of EBD, 5, 16–17, 24, 25, 26, 30,
    31–32, 38, 39–40, 48–50, 60,
    63–64
  of EH, 71, 75, 76–77
  of ELL, 63–64, 82, 83, 84, 86, 91
  of EMR, 5, 10, 82, 83, 84, 86, 91
  and falling between the cracks, 113
  and family/parents, 24, 36, 64–65
  of gifted, 30, 31–32
  and IQ, 10
  of LD, 5, 12–14, 16–17, 38, 39–40,
    48–50, 60, 63–64, 71, 75, 76–
    77, 92, 93–94, 109
  and norms, 10

Assessment/evaluation (*continued*)
  for TMH, 91
  variability and subjectivity in, 6
  See also Tests
Attendance, 24, 39, 60, 80, 84, 92–
  98, 99–107, 108
Austin (case study), 46–54, 60

Bartholomew (case study), 87–91
Basic psychological processes,
  definition of, 12
Beery-Buktenica Development Test of
  Visual Motor Integration, 100
Behavior
  acting-out, 70
  and ADHD, 22, 23, 24–25, 26, 28,
    72–74, 75
  and assessment, 16
  and behavior modification, 54–55
  and continuum of disabilities, 3, 4, 8
  and EBD, 22–26, 28, 29, 30–36, 39,
    41–43, 44, 47–48, 50, 52–56,
    58, 59, 60, 62, 64, 66–67, 69–
    70
  and EH, 72–74, 75
  and ELL, 62, 64, 66–67, 69–70, 85
  and EMR, 85
  and gifted, 29, 30–31, 32, 33–34,
    35, 36
  and LD, 39, 41–43, 44, 47–48, 50,
    52, 53, 54–56, 58, 59, 60, 62,
    64, 66–67, 69–70, 72–74, 75,
    92, 95, 96, 108, 109, 112
  management of, 17, 54–56, 66–67,
    69–70
  and physical intimidation/restraint,
    67, 69
  and referrals, 5
  responses to management of, 69–70
  in restrictive environments, 66–67
  and tyranny of the norm, 117
  See also Discipline; *specific case
    study*
Bender Visual Motor Gestalt Test, 49,
  77, 84, 100

Bilingual Curriculum Content (BCC),
  88–89, 90
Brown v. Board of Education (1954), 9
Busing, 33, 46, 54, 60, 65, 84

Case studies
  absence, 92–98, 99–107
  ADHD, 21–28, 71–78
  Anita, 99–107
  Austin, 46–40
  Bartholomew, 87–91
  between the cracks, 113–16
  Clementina, 79–86
  EBD, 21–28, 29–37, 38–45, 46–40,
    61–70
  Edith, 61–70
  EH, 71–78
  ELL, 61–70, 79–86, 87–91
  EMR, 79–86, 87–91
  Germaine, 38–45
  gifted, 29–37
  ignored student, 79–86, 87–91
  Kanita, 29–37
  LD, 38–45, 46–60, 61–70, 71–78,
    92–98, 99–107, 108–12
  low achiever, 108–12
  Marc, 108–12
  Matthew, 46–40
  Miles, 92–98
  Paul, 71–78
  Robert, 21–28
  sensitivity, 38–45
  Taddeus, 113–16
Class size
  and ADHD, 22
  and EBD, 22, 33, 40, 43, 44, 45, 48,
    50, 52, 54, 60
  and ELL, 88, 89
  and EMR, 88, 89
  and gifted, 33
  and LD, 40, 42, 44, 45, 48, 50, 52,
    54, 60, 94
  and referrals, 6
Clementina (case study), 79–86
Consistency, use of, 55

Counseling, 35, 40, 53, 66
Cramer, Elizabeth, chapters by, 46–60, 99–107
Cross, C., 4, 8, 11, 13, 14
CST (child study team), 6, 24, 27, 71–78, 82, 86, 93, 113

Darling-Hammond, L., 117
Definition
  dilemmas of, 9, 12–14, 15–16
  See also specific disability or term
Desegregation, 46, 60
Diagnostic and Statistical Manual of Mental Disorders (DSM-IV), 3–4, 78
Disabilities
  categories of, 3–5, 8–17
  continuum of, 3, 4–5, 8
  definition of, 3
  and disproportionate representation of race/ethnicity, 4, 8, 11, 17, 46, 117
  function of labeling of, 78
  medically-diagnosed, 4
  multiple, 87–91
  need for rethinking concept of, 117
  as socially constructed concept, 3–7, 9
  stigma of, 4
  See also specific disability
Discipline, 23, 28, 30, 42, 43, 56–58, 66–67, 69–70, 79. See also Behavior
Discrepancy model, 13
Donovan, S., 4, 8, 11, 13, 14
Dropouts, 15

EBD (emotional/behavioral disorder)
  and academic issues, 25, 26, 40, 41, 43, 48, 49, 50, 53, 54, 55, 56–60, 62, 63, 68–69, 72, 77
  and ADHD, 15, 21–28, 71–78
  assessment of, 5, 16–17, 24, 25, 26, 30, 31–32, 38, 39, 48–50, 60, 63–64, 71, 75, 76–77, 85

  and behavior, 22–26, 28, 29, 30–36, 39, 41–43, 44, 47–48, 50, 52–56, 58, 59, 60, 62, 64, 66–67, 69–70, 72–74, 75
  case studies about, 21–28, 29–37, 38–45, 46–60, 71–78
  as category of disability, 3, 4, 14–17
  definition of, 15–17, 28, 36, 70, 78
  and ELL, 12, 61–70
  and gifted, 29–37
  increase in identification of, 14–15
  and instruction, 17, 22, 23, 42, 51, 56–59, 61, 67, 68–69
  and IQ, 25, 31, 32, 49, 50, 77
  and LD, 15, 16–17, 38–45, 46–60, 61–70, 71–78
  placement for, 5, 7, 14, 17, 24, 25–26, 27, 28, 29, 30, 33–35, 36–37, 42, 45, 49–60, 61, 62, 65–68, 70, 71–72, 75, 76–78
  questions about, 28, 60, 70
  and race/ethnicity, 4, 14–15, 17, 22, 28, 60
  referrals for, 5, 30, 31, 33, 36, 48–50, 60, 62–63, 71, 72, 74–75, 77
  in restricted environment, 66–67, 78
  and retention/promotion, 22, 24, 30, 38, 44
  and schedule, 67–68
  and sensitivity, 38–45
  stigma attached to, 15, 17, 36–37, 54, 78
  and tests, 35, 39, 43, 45, 48, 49, 50, 60, 62, 63, 68, 76–77
Edith (case study), 16, 61–70
Education for All Handicapped Children's Act (EHA) (1975), 9, 12, 15
ELL (English-language learner)
  and academic issues, 62, 63, 68–69, 83–84, 85, 87, 88, 89, 90–91
  and ADHD, 78
  assessment of, 63–64, 82, 83, 84, 86, 91

ELL (English-language learner)
    (*continued*)
  and behavior, 62, 64, 66–67, 69–70,
    85
  case studies about, 79–86, 87–91
  and EBD, 61–70
  and EH, 78
  and EMR, 79–86, 87–91
  and family perspectives, 64–65
  and instruction, 61, 67, 68–69, 80,
    81
  and IQ, 83, 87–88
  and LD, 12, 61–70, 78
  placement for, 61, 62, 65–68, 70,
    79, 82–86, 88–90, 91
  questions about, 70, 86, 91
  referrals for, 62–63, 79, 82, 83, 86
  and retention/promotion, 80–81
  and schedule, 67–68
  and tests, 10, 62, 63, 68, 80–81, 83–
    84, 85, 87, 88
  See also ESOL
Emotional adaptation, 100
EMR (educable mental retardation)
  and academic issues, 11, 83–84, 85,
    87, 88, 89, 90–91
  and adaptive functioning, 10
  assessment of, 5, 10, 82, 83, 84, 86,
    91
  and behavior, 85
  case studies about, 79–86, 87–91
  as category of disability, 3, 8–11
  definition of, 9
  and ELL, 79–86, 87–91
  and instruction, 80, 81
  judgments about, 8–11
  labeling of, 84, 91
  and LD, 11, 13
  placement for, 5, 7, 10–11, 29, 79,
    82–86, 88–90, 91
  questions about, 86, 91
  and race/ethnicity, 4, 8, 9, 13
  referrals for, 5, 79, 82, 83, 86
  and retention/promotion, 80–81
  and tests, 80–81, 83–84, 85, 87, 88

ESOL (English for speakers of other
    languages), 22, 46, 61, 71, 77, 79,
    84, 88–89. *See also* ELL
Evaluation. *See* assessment/evaluation
Exclusionary clause, 13

Falling between the cracks, 8, 11, 113–
    16
Family/parents
  advocates for, 70, 86
  of Anita, 99–100, 101, 105–6, 107
  and assessment decisions, 6, 24, 36,
    64–65
  of Austin, 47, 53, 54
  of Bartholomew, 88, 89
  and behavior management, 69
  children's relationships with, 27, 33,
    35, 36, 44
  of Clementina, 79–80, 82, 83, 84–
    85
  criticisms of decisions/programs by,
    64–65, 105–6
  culture/religion of, 61, 62, 64, 70
  death of, 53, 54
  in difficult situations, 21
  as dysfunctional, 31, 32, 37, 79–80
  of Edith, 61, 62, 63, 64–65, 69–70
  of Germaine, 38, 39, 41, 44
  ignoring of, 82
  involvement of, 62, 65, 98, 109,
    110, 112–13
  of Kanita, 31, 33, 34, 35, 36, 37
  lack of understanding by, 66
  of Marc, 108–9, 110, 112–13
  of Matthew, 47, 56, 60
  of Miles, 93, 94, 95–96, 98
  of Paul, 72, 73, 74, 75, 76, 77, 78
  and placement, 7, 27–28, 33, 34, 35,
    36, 65–66, 83, 84–85, 86, 88,
    89
  as problems, 99–100
  and referrals, 6, 30
  and retention/promotion, 38
  rights of, 82, 86
  of Robert, 24, 26–28

and school choice, 106, 107
school personnel's relationships
    with, 27, 30, 70, 107, 113
of Taddeus, 113
See also specific case study
FAPE (free appropriate public
    education), 10
Florida, 11, 14
Freedom from Distractibility subscale,
    32
Fuchs, L., 12

General education
  and ADHD, 25–26, 75
  and attendance, 102–3
  and EBD, 17, 25–26, 34–35, 41, 46–
    47, 50–52, 53, 54, 62
  and EH, 75
  and ELL, 62, 80, 81, 91
  and EMR, 80, 81, 91
  and gifted, 34–35
  and LD, 41, 46–47, 50–52, 53, 54,
    62, 75, 101, 102–3, 107, 109–11
  See also Placement
Germaine (case study), 16, 38–45
Gifted
  assessment of, 30, 31–32
  and behavior, 30–31, 32, 33–34, 35,
    36
  case study about, 29–37
  definition of, 36
  and EBD, 29–37
  historical concept of, 4
  and IQ, 31, 32
  placement for, 30, 33–35, 36–37
  referrals for, 30, 31, 33, 36
  and retention/promotion, 30
  and tests, 31–32, 35
Gramsci, A., 117

Harry, B., 4–5, 28, 37
Hart, Juliet E.
  chapter by, 61–70
  references to works by, 26, 28, 36,
    37, 70

Harvey, K., 10
Health/medical issues, 69, 80, 91, 93, 101
Home Language Arts (HLA), 88–89,
    90
Homework, 51, 53, 54, 60, 72, 76,
    112, 113
Hosp, J. L., 16
House-Tree-Person Test, 49, 100

IDEA (Individuals with Disabilities
    Education Improvement Act), 3,
    4, 7, 10, 12, 13, 15, 28, 91
Identity, and placement, 7
IEP (individualized education
    program)
  for Bartholomew, 88, 89
  for Clementina, 84
  for Edith, 70
  for Germaine, 40, 41, 44
  for Kanita, 34, 35, 37
  for Miles, 95, 96
  and multiple disabilities, 91
  and placement decisions, 7
  for Robert, 25
Ignored, students as, 47–48, 51
  case studies about, 79–86, 87–91
Instruction
  and ADHD, 22, 23
  and climate of schools, 109
  and EBD, 17, 22, 23, 42, 51, 56–59,
    61, 67, 68–69
  and ELL, 61, 67, 68–69, 80, 81
  and EMR, 80, 81
  and falling between the cracks, 116
  and LD, 42, 51, 56–59, 61, 67, 68–
    69, 111
  in special education, 5, 56–59
IQ
  and ADHD, 25, 77
  and assessment, 10
  and definitions of disabilities, 9
  and EBD, 25, 31, 32, 49, 50
  and EH, 77
  and ELL, 83, 87–88
  and EMR, 83, 87–88

IQ (*continued*)
  and gifted, 31, 32
  and LD, 11, 12, 14, 49, 50, 77, 94,
    100, 105, 109
  validity and appropriateness of tests
    of, 10

"Judgment" categories, 8–17. *See also
  specific category*

Kanita (case study), 29–37
Kauffman (K-ABC) test, 88
Kinetic Family Drawing Test, 49, 77, 100
King-Sears, P., 12
Klingner, J., 4–5, 28, 37

Larry P. v. Riles, 9
LD (learning disorders)
  and academic issues, 11, 13, 14, 40,
    41, 43, 48, 49, 50, 53, 54, 55,
    56–60, 62, 63, 68–69, 72, 77,
    93, 94, 95, 100, 101, 102, 104,
    105, 109, 111
  and ADHD, 15, 71–78
  assessment of, 5, 12–14, 16–17, 38,
    39, 48–50, 60, 63–64, 71, 75,
    76–77, 92, 93–94, 109
  or attendance, 92–98, 99–107
  and behavior, 39, 41–43, 44, 47–
    48, 50, 52, 53, 54, 55–56, 59,
    60, 62, 64, 66–67, 69–70, 72–
    74, 75, 92, 95, 96, 108, 109,
    112
  case studies about, 38–45, 46–60,
    71–78, 92–98, 99–107, 108–12
  as category of disability, 3, 11–14
  criteria for identification of, 12–13
  definition of, 12–14, 78, 107
  and EBD, 15, 16–17, 38–45, 46–60,
    61–70, 78
  and EH, 71–78
  and ELL, 12, 61–70, 78
  and EMR, 11, 13
  and family perspectives, 64–65
  home effects on, 96–97
  increase in identification of, 11–12

  and instruction, 42, 51, 56–59, 61,
    67, 68–69, 111
  and IQ, 11, 12, 14, 49, 50, 77, 94,
    100, 105, 109
  and low achievers, 108–12
  and LRE, 14
  placement for, 5, 8, 11, 14, 29, 42,
    45, 49–60, 61, 62, 65–68, 70,
    71–72, 75, 76–78, 94–96, 97,
    101, 102–4, 109–11
  questions about, 60, 70, 78, 97–98,
    107, 111–12
  and race/ethnicity, 4, 8, 11–12, 13, 60
  referrals for, 5, 15–16, 48–50, 60,
    62–63, 71, 72, 74–75, 77, 92,
    93–94, 100, 101, 109–11, 112
  and restricted environment, 66–67
  and retention/promotion, 38, 44,
    94–96, 97, 100–101, 105
  and schedule, 67–68
  and sensitivity, 38–45
  and social issues, 101–2
  and tests, 39, 43, 45, 48, 49, 50, 60,
    62, 63, 68, 75, 76–77, 94, 100,
    109
Low achievers, 11, 108–12
LRE (least restrictive environment), 7,
    10, 14, 17, 88–89, 91

MacMillan, D. L., 9
Mainstreaming
  and assessment, 10
  and dilemmas of placement, 10
  and EBD, 34–35, 55, 59, 60, 68
  and ELL, 68, 91
  and EMR, 91
  and gifted, 34–35
  and LD, 55, 59, 60, 68, 95
  and LRE, 10
Manifest determination, 28
Marc (case study), 108–12
Mariga, L., 10
Matthew (case study), 46–50, 54–60
Medications, 23, 24, 26, 28, 73, 75
Mercer, A. R., 12
Mercer, C. D., 12

Miles (case study), 92–98
MR (mental retardation), 9, 10–11, 86

National Academy of Sciences, 4, 8
Native Americans, 4, 11, 14
Needs, and assessment decisions, 6
No Child Left Behind Act, 97
Norms/normalcy, 3, 5, 8, 10, 11, 117

Office of Special Education Programs, 10
OHI (other health impaired), 4, 25
"Opportunity to learn," 5, 28

Parents. *See* family/parents; *specific case study*
Paul (case study), 71–78
PDKs (pretty dumb kids), 115–16
Peers, 26, 42, 44, 50, 52, 56, 62, 64, 70, 72, 80, 95, 101–2
Physical intimidation/restraint, 67, 69
Placement
    and ADHD, 24, 25–26, 27, 28, 71–72, 75, 76–78
    and attendance, 103–4
    concerns about decisions of, 6–7
    and continuum of disabilities, 4–5
    dilemmas of, 10–11, 14, 17
    for EBD, 5, 7, 14, 17, 24, 25–26, 27, 28, 29, 30, 33–34, 35, 36–37, 42, 45, 49–60, 61, 62, 65–68, 70
    for EH, 71–72, 75, 76–78
    for ELL, 61, 62, 65–68, 70, 79, 82–86, 88–90, 91
    for EMR, 5, 7, 10–11, 29, 79, 82–86, 88–90, 91
    exit rate from, 7
    and family/parents, 7, 27–28, 33, 34, 35, 36, 65–66, 84–85, 86, 88, 89
    and gifted, 30, 33–34, 35, 36–37
    and identity, 7
    for LD, 5, 8, 11, 14, 29, 42, 45, 49–60, 61, 62, 65–68, 70, 71–72, 75, 76–78, 94–96, 97, 101, 102–4, 109–11

and low achievers, 109–11
and MR, 10–11
part-time or self-contained, 7, 25–26
rates of, 29, 46
See also General education; LRE; Mainstreaming; Special education
Post, L., 117
Promotion. *See* Retention/promotion
Psychologists, 6, 7. *See also* Assessment/evaluation; CST
Pull-out programs, 112

Questions
    about ADHD, 28, 78
    and attendance, 97–98, 107
    about EBD, 28, 36–37, 40, 60, 70
    about EH, 78
    about ELL, 70, 86, 91
    about EMR, 86, 91
    and falling between the cracks, 116
    and gifted, 36–37
    about LD, 44, 60, 70, 78, 97–98, 107, 111–12

Race/ethnicity
    and ADHD, 22, 28
    as disproportionally in special education, 4, 8, 11, 17, 46, 117
    and EBD, 4, 14–15, 17, 22, 28, 60
    and EMR, 4, 8, 9, 13
    and LD, 4, 8, 11–12, 13, 60
    and norms, 17, 117
    and placement decisions, 7
    and referrals, 46
    stereotyping of, 28
Referrals
    and academic issues, 5
    and ADHD, 23–25, 71, 72, 74–75, 77
    decisions about, 5–6
    delays in, 83–86
    for EBD, 5, 23–25, 30, 31, 33, 36, 48–50, 60, 62–63
    for EH, 71, 72, 74–75, 77
    for ELL, 62–63, 79, 82, 83, 86

Referrals (*continued*)
  for EMR, 5, 79, 82, 86
  and falling between the cracks, 113
  family/parents reactions to, 6, 30
  and gifted, 30, 31, 33, 36
  lack of standard criteria for, 5
  for LD, 5, 15–16, 48–50, 60, 62–63,
      71, 72, 74–75, 77, 92, 93–94,
      100, 101, 109–11, 112
  and low achievers, 109–11
  monitoring process for, 112
  patterns of, 5–6
  and race/ethnicity, 46
  rates of, 5–6
  as scientific or arbitrary, 48–50
  and teachers' perceptions, 62–63
  variability in process for, 5–6
Reschly, D. J., 9, 16
Response to intervention (RTI), 12,
    112
Restrictive environment, 11, 60, 66–
    68
Retention/promotion
  and ADHD, 22, 24
  and EBD, 22, 24, 30, 38, 44
  and ELL, 80–81
  and EMR, 80–81
  and falling between the cracks, 113,
      116
  and gifted, 30
  and LD, 38, 44, 94–96, 97, 100–
      101, 105
  social, 97
Robert (case study), 21–28, 113
Roberts Apperception Test, 32

Scales of Independent Behavior (SIB),
    88
Schedule, 67–68, 104–5
Schools
  choice of, 106, 107
  climate of, 4, 21, 29, 38, 46, 54, 61,
      66, 109
  reputation of, 6
  transfers to other, 26, 29, 54, 65,
      66, 106

Sensitivity, 38–45, 47
Serpell, R., 10
SLD (specific learning disabilities), 3,
    12, 97. *See also* LD
SM (socially maladjusted), 15
Social issues
  and LD, 101–2
  See also Behavior
Special education
  and ADHD, 25, 26, 71–72, 75, 78
  and attendance, 103–4
  borderline cases needing, 97
  cancellation of, 103, 106
  criteria for qualification for, 78
  and dilemmas of placement, 10–11
  and EBD, 25, 26, 31, 33–34, 36, 38,
      40–41, 43, 44, 45, 50, 53, 54–
      60, 65–66
  and EH, 71–72, 75, 78
  and ELL, 65–66, 82–84, 85–86, 89–
      90
  and EMR, 82–84, 85–86, 89–90
  exiting from, 36
  and falling between the cracks, 116
  and gifted, 31, 33–34, 36
  instruction in, 5, 56–59
  and LD, 13, 38, 40–41, 43, 44, 45,
      50, 53, 54–60, 65–66, 71–72,
      75, 78, 92, 94–96, 97, 100–
      107, 109, 111, 112
  and parental involvement, 112
  primary or intermediate, 40–41
  race/ethnicity disproportionally
      represented in, 17, 46, 117
  scheduling of, 67–68, 104–5
  social forces concerning placement
      in, 7
  and statewide tests, 44
  and stigma of disabilities, 5
  See also Placement; *specific case
      study*
Speech impairment, 87, 88, 89–90, 91
Sturges, Keith, chapters by, 46–60, 99–
    107
Success for All (reading program), 102,
    103

Suicide, statements about, 63, 64, 65
Suspension/expulsion, 11, 24, 26, 59

Taddeus (case study), 113–16
Tests
  and ADHD, 24, 76–77
  bias and subjectivity of, 16
  and EBD, 16, 24, 31–32, 35, 39,
    43, 45, 48, 49, 50, 60, 62,
    63, 68
  and EH, 76–77
  and ELL, 10, 62, 63, 68, 80–81, 83–
    84, 85, 87, 88
  and EMR, 80–81, 83–84, 85, 87,
    88
  and gifted, 31–32, 35
  and LD, 39, 43, 45, 48, 49, 50, 60,
    62, 63, 68, 75, 76–77, 94, 100,
    109
  projective, 31–32, 49, 50, 62

  statewide, 6, 35, 60, 68, 80–81
  See also Assessment/evaluation;
    specific test
TMH (trainable mentally
  handicapped), 91
Tyrese (Robert's friend), 22, 23–24

U.S. Department of Education, 12, 13,
  14–15, 17

Vaughn, S., 12
Vocational and Rehabilitation Act, 4

Wechsler Individual Achievement Test
  (WIAT), 77
Wechsler Intelligence Scales for
  Children (WISC III), 31, 32, 40,
  49, 76, 83, 94, 100
Woodcock Johnson Tests of
  Achievement, 32, 43, 49, 100, 109

About the Authors

Beth Harry, Ph.D., is a professor of special education in the Department of Teaching and Learning at the University of Miami, Florida. She was a co-principal investigator on the research project on which these case studies were based. Her research and teaching focus on the impact of special education on culturally and linguistically diverse families and children. She served as a member of the National Academy of Sciences' panel to study ethnic disproportionality in special education in 2002, and is currently a co-principal investigator for The National Center for Culturally Responsive Educational Systems (NCCRESt). In 2003 she received a Fulbright award to do research on Moroccan children's schooling in Spain. Dr. Harry, a native of Jamaica, entered the field of special education as a parent of a child with cerebral palsy.

Janette Klingner, Ph.D., is an associate professor in bilingual special education at the University of Colorado, Boulder, in the Division for Educational Equity and Cultural Diversity. She was a co-principal investigator on the research project on which these case studies were based. Dr. Klingner was a bilingual special education teacher for 10 years before earning her doctorate in reading and learning disabilities from the University of Miami. Currently she is a co-principal investigator for The National Center for Culturally Responsive Educational Systems (NCCRESt). A research focus of hers is the disproportionate representation of culturally and linguistically diverse students in special education. In 2004 she won AERA's Early Career Award.

Elizabeth Cramer, Ph.D., is an assistant professor of special education in the Department of Educational and Psychological Studies at Florida International University in Miami. She was a graduate assistant on the research project on which these case studies are based. She served as a secondary special education teacher before completing her Ph.D. in reading and special education at the University of Miami in 2002. Her areas of teaching and research include preparing urban teachers to instruct culturally and linguistically diverse children with exceptionalities to effectively access the general education curriculum. She currently serves as a principal investigator or co-principal investigator on over $2.4 million worth of grants aimed at achieving this objective.

Keith M. Sturges is an educational anthropologist and doctoral candidate in Cultural Studies in Education at The University of Texas–Austin. He was the coordinator of the research project on which these case studies were based. His interests include planned school change, dismantling privileged education policy and practice, and critical ethnography. Currently, he is researching program evaluation as cultural production.

Robert F. Moore, Ed.D., is an associate professor of special education in the Department of Teaching and Learning at the University of Miami, Florida. He is coordinator of the Undergraduate Teacher Preparation Program in Special Education. He served as the primary consultant to the research project on which these case studies were based. He has worked extensively on accreditation matters with the Commission on Colleges of the Southern Association of Colleges and Schools, and is currently serving as project investigator for a grant from Florida's Critical Jobs Initiative–SUCCEED program.